Dancing on the Graves of Your Past

Support Group Leader's Guide

Yvonne Martinez

Dancing on the Graves of Your Past ~ Support Group Leader's Guide

Dancing on the Graves of Your Past Support Group Leader's Guide

Copyright © 2010 by Yvonne Martinez

All rights reserved

This book is protected by the copyright law of the United States of America.

Permission is granted to reproduce "forms and handouts" solely for the purpose of group ministry.

No portion of this book may be copied or reprinted for gain or profit.

Unless otherwise noted, all Scripture quotations are from

the Holy Bible,
New International Version. Copyright © 1973, 1978, 1984,

International Bible Society. Used by permission of Zondervan.

All rights reserved.

The "NIV" and "New International Version" trademarks are registered in the United States Patent and Trademark Office by International

Bible Society. Use of either trademark requires the permission of

International Bible Society.

ISBN is 1453820973

EAN-13 is 9781453820971

Printed in the United States of America

Published and Distributed by Stillwater Lavender

www.StillwaterLavender.com

**Your group may qualify for
book and workbook discounts.**

Dancing on the Graves of Your Past Support Group Leader's Guide

Dancing on the Graves of Your Past Support Group Leader's Guide is a hands-on ministry tool teaching you how to build, maintain, and facilitate group ministry for hurting people.

Learn all the practical information needed to start a support group ministry with emotional and spiritual guidelines to help you set the captives free.

- How Ministries are Birthed
- Why Begin a Group
- How to Get Started
- Forms Your Group will Need
- A 10 Week Format with Group Curriculum
- How to Handle Conflicts and Difficult People

Includes leader's copy of *Dancing on the Graves of Your Past* book and workbook

Leader's Workshops Available

Table of Contents

Introduction		**7**
Chapter 1	How Ministries are Birthed	**11**
Chapter 2	Why Begin a Group	**21**
Chapter 3	Getting Started	**35**
Chapter 4	Week 1 - Welcome	**49**
Chapter 5	Week 2 – The Past	**59**
Chapter 6	Week 3 – The Invitation	**77**
Chapter 7	Week 4 - Old Music	**101**
Chapter 8	Week 5 - Old Dances	**133**
Chapter 9	Week 6 - Dance of Surrender	**152**
Chapter 10	Week 7 - Dance of Forgiveness	**182**
Chapter 11	Week 8 - Dance of the Overcomer	**219**
Chapter 12	Week 9 - Dance of the Kingdom	**253**
Chapter 13	Week 10 - Dance Face to Face	**269**
Chapter 14	Handling Conflicts and Difficult People	**289**
Chapter 15	The End is a Beginning	**307**
Appendix	Forms and Handouts	**309**

Introduction

Dancing on the Graves of Your Past Support Group Leader's Guide is a hands-on guide to teach you how to build, maintain, and facilitate a Christian support group ministry to those who are hurting emotionally. It is written as a ministry leadership guide and companion to Dancing on the Graves of Your Past book and Experience the Journey Workbook

By reading this guide and following the instructions, you will learn all the practical information needed to start a support group ministry, as well as learn emotional and spiritual guidelines to help you understand and relate to the group participants.

Included is information about:
- **How Ministries are Birthed**
- **Why Begin a Group**
- **How to Get Started**
- **Forms Your Group will Need**
- **A 10 Week Group Curriculum**
- **How to Handle Conflicts and Difficult People**

Discover how you, too, can help others who are hurting emotionally. Join Christian leaders across the nation who are successfully using Yvonne Martinez' ministry material, Dancing on the Graves of Your Past, in a support group setting.

"In the plan of the Great Dance plans without number interlock, and each movement becomes in its season the breaking into flower of the whole design to which all else had been directed. Thus each is equally at the centre and none are there by being equals, but some by giving place and some by receiving it, the small things by their smallness and the great by their greatness, and all the patterns linked and looped together by the unions of a kneeling with a sceptred love. Blessed be He!"
C.S. Lewis, Perelandra, excerpt from pp. 218-219

1

How Ministries are Birthed

*"I pray also that the eyes of your heart may be
enlightened in order that you may know the hope to which he has called you,
the riches of his glorious inheritance in the saints, and his incomparably
great power for us who believe."*

— Eph. 1: 18

My heart heard the words from Romans 6:28, "And we know that in all things God works for the good of those who love Him, who have been called according to His purpose," (NIV) as I sat and listened to the women in our new group.

A common thread wove through their tragic testimonials of physical abuse, sexual abuse, emotional neglect, rejection and loss. They were all victims, stuck in a pattern of thinking and not knowing their choices. They all carried emotional scars from their past circumstances. These wounds never healed and became little cancers that ate away at their hope and future. Their backgrounds varied but their helplessness to change didn't.

And me? It was 1985 and I was the new group facilitator, launched into counseling and group ministry because I had a heart for others who had gone through similar circumstances to mine.

My story included much of the same trauma as theirs except one thing was different. My story had a happy ending. The pain from my past no longer breathed down my neck and hung around my heels. Yesterday was no longer today's prison. I felt ready for the challenge but needed assurance I really had something to offer to others.

Through the story of the Samaritan woman in the Gospel of John, I found the courage to reach out to others. She was a woman of disputable character who became the first evangelist in Samaria. I would like to introduce you to her and the four elements she taught me about birthing a ministry.

Ministry Opportunity is Planted Within the Disappointments of Life

It wasn't unusual for Jewish travelers to take the long road around Samaria since Jews had nothing to do with Samaritans. Samaritans were considered a low class of people, a Judeo-Gentile race, a vulgar word in the mouth of a Jew. Samaritan women were equal only to that of a slave, to be unseen and unheard, especially in the presence of a man.

Today, like everyday, this Samaritan woman carried her heavy water jug to the well for water. Her physical countenance displayed the emotional burden she carried. Her head hung low as she reminisced over her life. Rejection plagued her thoughts as depression overwhelmed her. She had been married five times and was now living with a man.

History neglects to record too much else about her personal past. In fact, the Bible never even calls her by name. I believe that is because she could be anyone of us.

She had no idea today was going to be different. Despite her empty-looking future, God had a plan for her. Certainly, in the minds of others, she was an outcast, a prostitute, a tramp. How could anyone looking at her situation believe there could be redemption for her sins? Who would suspect life would turn around for her? Her family and friends did not value her or believe in her, but God did.

What no one else knew, except God, was that beside the Samaritan woman's life and mine was a sign that stated:

"Testimony in Progress - God at Work"

Within each tragedy, failure, and disappointment was ministry's potential waiting to sprout forth. The same unseen sign has been posted beside your trials and tragedies, too.

Ministry Opportunity is Watered With our Tears

She went to the well at noon to draw water, even though temperatures soared high at that time of day. She was a woman with a bad reputation, so she made her daily trip to the well when no one would be there. She didn't want others to look at her or gossip about her.

Five marriages must have left her broken and wounded. Did she cry herself to sleep at night? Was she full of fear and doubt? She was waiting for the Messiah, but when would He come? Her tears watered faith and hope. Each tear surrender her failures into God's hands, praying for an answer. Tears of desperation and repentance will turn God's head.

Ministry Opportunity is Grown With the Revelation of Who Jesus Is

We are not much different. How many times has Jesus passed by us and we didn't recognize Him? How many times has He talked to us and we didn't hear Him?

And then, when He offered a genuine interest in her, she saw that this was the Messiah. He quenched a life-long thirst for love and security. The revelation of who Jesus really was changed her forever.

Jesus purposed to go through Samaria, the same as He purposed to come to my town and yours. He broke all traditional customs to meet her that day. He did not want a religious experience with her. He wanted a relationship. He wants a relationship with us, too.

Ministry is Birthed the Moment We Give Someone Jesus

Leaving behind her old identity, she dropped the jug and ran throughout the village, inviting people to come meet Jesus, the Man who spoke the words of life to her. Her head was no longer down; her eyes no longer filled with depression. She was a new creation. Her life was renewed and people recognized the change in her. The moment she shared with them, her ministry was birthed.

The Samaritan woman's testimony became her credential to minister to others. You and I do not need degrees or diplomas either. We just need to bring others to meet Jesus.

The first time I was asked to give my testimony, I was attending a small church that was filled with saintly-looking Christians. The pastor's wife said, "God told me to ask you to speak for the ladies group!" I thought that was pretty official, but how could I sit in front of the women in this church and bare my dirty laundry?

My mind filled with questions. Would my testimony bring glory to God or just promote gossip? Was God really healing me? I had been asking God to use me, hadn't I? I wanted to share, but I wasn't sure if I was ready to reveal my past.

A few weeks after a "gulp" and a "yes" and a prayer, I was sitting in front of six neat and proper Christian women. My notes were neatly typed and outlined. It was a good thing because my hands were shaking enough to distort even the best penmanship. Prayerfully, I began recounting my testimony and the healing God was bringing.

My listeners' eyes seemed to be glued to every word I spoke. Some would look down in horror; others had tears in their eyes. I was filled with doubts, more concerned with their reaction than with my speech. I couldn't tell if they were feeling sorry for me, leveling judgments, or could they possibly relate to me.

At the close I asked them to pray with me. They all bowed their heads and closed their eyes. I challenged them by asking, "Can any of you relate in any way to what I have shared?" They all raised their hands. Encouraged,

I asked another question, "Do any of you have unresolved circumstances or feelings from your past that you would like to bring to Jesus for healing?" I closed my eyes, thinking to myself, "Yvonne, these women don't have any problems. They are mature. They have it all together. You've dropped the ball now!" But to my amazement, when I opened my eyes, all six women had their hands raised as Kleenex wiped noses and the tears rolling down their cheeks. My heart leaped for joy. At that moment, God spoke reassurance and love to me. He had really used my broken life to reach out to these ladies. I had something to give. I could give them Jesus.

Ministry was a simple prayer. I asked each woman to take her unopened box, full of hurt and disappointment, and open it before Jesus. After a few moments of silence, we gave the contents to Him through prayer, asking Him to refill the box with His love and grace.

I learned a lot that evening about the women before me. Three had been sexually abused, one was a recent widow, one had never dealt with the death of a child, and one had never forgiven her husband for leaving her. They weren't perfect. They hurt just like I did.

I learned something about my relationship with God, too. He stayed by my side. He was faithful. I had to ask forgiveness for doubting Him and judging others.

The next time I gave my testimony was at a Women's Aglow Fellowship. I fasted, prayed, and cried before God. Then I found out the attendance was a record high of 120 women! My nervousness turned to sheer panic as I hid in the rest room, waiting for the meeting to begin. I prayed I wouldn't pass out while standing before them.

At the end, 80 women came forward for prayer. He touched their lives and mine that morning. He was birthing a ministry and giving me a glimpse of how He was working "good" from the misery of my life.

The woman at the well evangelized Samaria with her testimony and revival broke forth. This great outpouring of God's Holy Spirit is attributed to the woman at the well, who began as a mission field and ended as a missionary.

What trials and triumphs have you been through?

_____
_____
_____
_____
_____
_____
_____
_____
_____
_____
_____

Review the list on the following pages and circle those areas in which you have experienced some element of healing.

Depression	Stress	Mid-Life Crisis
Alcoholism	Co-Dependency	Drug Addiction
Eating Disorder	Phobias	Abandonment
Suicide	Homosexuality	Weight Control
Exercise	Nutrition	Church Administration
Teaching	Evangelism	Prayer
Lay Counseling	Cult Exposure	Friendship
Singles	Widowhood	Loneliness
Rejection	Betrayal	General Advice
Unsaved Spouse	False Religion	Marriage Enrichment
Premarital Counseling	Discipline	Adoption/Foster Parent
Premature Birth	Miscarriage/Death	Single Parent
Daycare	Empty Nest	Nest Too Full
Communication	Teenage Pregnancy	Abortion
Step-Parenting	In-Laws	Elderly
Handicapped	Long Term Illness	Divorce
Separation	Victim Assistance	Counseling
Remarriage	Death and Dying	Coping
Spousal Abuse	Rape	Molestation/Incest
Verbal Abuse	Prison	Personality
Self-image	Infidelity	Boundaries
Establishing Priorities	Femininity	Leader Development

Education/Training	Public Speaking	Working Mothers
Bible Study	STD and Promiscuity	Immorality
Hospitality	Other:	Other:

How many areas were you able to select? _____

Each category you checked could be developed into a ministry. When I review my "Testimony in Progress," I am astounded at all the ministry opportunities I have, too! Now, look at how many of your experiences could be encouraging to others in a support group setting.

A frequent question at this point is, "Do I have to be healed before God can use me?" Let us look again at the Samaritan woman.

The Bible never records that every aspect of her life was healed when she went running through the town inviting people to meet Jesus. Her experience with receiving Jesus as Lord was the greatest testimony she had. Her ministry developed and grew as did her relationship with Him.

I am certainly more emotionally healthy today than when I first shared my testimony, and if I had waited to be perfect, I would not be writing this book! Ministry grows as we trust Him with our personal and spiritual growth.

We do need to be sure we are leading people in the right direction — to Jesus. You can only bring people as far as you have come yourself. However far that is, it is a testimony to the power of Christ that He has brought you that far. Remember, a personal testimony on any topic is the most powerful witnessing tool you own. We will discuss more about leadership in later chapters.

God used the misery of my life as stepping stones to ministry. We comfort others by our experience and challenge others through our hope.

2

Why Begin a Group?

"Praise be to the God and Father of our Lord Jesus Christ, the Father of compassion and the God of all comfort, who comforts us in all our troubles, so that we can comfort those in any trouble with the comfort we have received from God."

—2 Corinthians 1:3-4

According to the dictionary, a group is, "an assemblage of persons; two or more that make a unit; individuals or things considered together because of certain similarities," (American Heritage, 1976).

With this definition in mind, let us look at some group examples with which you may already be familiar.

You were born into a group called a family. Basketball and soccer activities are played in groups. A band is a group of musicians. Our government consists of varied groups, all serving different purposes.

As you can see, the concept of a group is not new. Looking to the Bible we also see examples. The Israelites were a large group of people traveling from Egypt, and Noah had quite a group with him on the Ark!

The most influential group we can learn from is the twelve men who were called and commissioned by Jesus. They followed Jesus' directions to go into all the earth, teaching people to obey everything He commanded (Matt. 28:18-20). These disciples established the groups we now call "church."

This is probably the best reason to begin a group. Small groups were a part of God's plan by which we, as Christians, would "grow in the grace and knowledge of our Lord and Savior, Jesus Christ," (2 Peter 3:18, NIV).

A support group (large or small) brings emotional, physical, and spiritual sustenance to individuals that come together to share common concerns and explore possible solutions. This is the essence of a support group.

The Value to Others

As we have seen, groups exist to serve many purposes. We will be looking at group ministries that serve as encouragement and healing to people with specific needs. Whether your group is to help the divorced, the adopted, or the abused, there are similar feelings all members may face.

Let me begin by giving you my definition of a victim. A victim is a person stuck in a pattern of thinking, believing he has no choices.

Usually we label someone a victim because he was violated in some way. Actually, a rape, a divorce, or abusive words are descriptions of what happened. How the person responds to what happened is what makes him a victim. The response can perpetuate even more heartache than the original event. I call the bonding with the past a type of "dance" relationship.

I could have women who were sexually molested, women who were raised with alcoholic parents, and women who live with verbally abusive husbands all in the same group. The events were different, but their feelings of rejection, worthlessness, and betrayal were the same. Both physical assault and verbal rejection can create equally painful and damaging responses.

Support groups consist of people who do not have the physical, emotional, and/or spiritual resources to move beyond their abuse, trauma or emotional pain. They do not know the steps to a dance of freedom with the Lord.

The following sentences describe some underlying beliefs of those who may attend your group:

— **No matter how hard I try, some part of me feels like I didn't try hard enough.**

— **No one, including God, could be happy with me, so I must find a way to change. But change is impossible.**

— **I feel safe when people ignore me.**

— **I hate myself when I have let someone down, even if it wasn't my fault.**

— I don't have the power to stand up to anyone, especially authority figures.

— If I must wait for something to happen, it will never happen. I don't deserve to be happy.

— I always feel guilty.

— People hurt me, so I can't trust anyone.

— No matter what I do, I should be doing something else.

— Whenever I reward myself, I overdo it or make wrong choices.

— My mind is always racing and I wonder why I behave like I do.

— There must be something really wrong with me.

There was a time when I could put my name by most of those sentences.

Can you relate to any of them? _____

A support group creates opportunity for hurting people to learn valuable information.

— **They are not alone in their feelings.**

— **They have choices to make about their circumstances.**

— **They can move forward beyond their pain.**

— **They can have healthy relationships.**

— **They can grow in relationship with Jesus.**

Would a support group have benefited you at some point in your life? Write a brief overview of what YOU needed.

_____
_____
_____
_____
_____
_____
_____
_____
_____

The Value to You

At the same time your group serves the needs of others, it will also challenge your personal growth. You may be faced with your own unresolved feelings as you move into the troubled lives of others.

This happens because no matter how far we have come in our own emotional healing, God never stops working on us. He tells us in Colossians 3:10, "... we are being renewed in knowledge in the image of our Creator," (NIV). This is a daily growing process.

Suzanne was a bright, energetic, young Christian woman. She had a heart for teenage girls who had post-abortion regrets so she began a closed group to meet the needs she saw. During the course of her group, she continually struggled with suppressing her own pain. Consequently, before the group was due to conclude Suzanne cancelled the group telling the girls she was not feeling well. She was embarrassed and felt like a failure.

Looking deeper into Suzanne's life, we found there were certain aspects of her own abortion she had not yet faced. Addressing these issues in the lives of others caused Suzanne extreme pain. In her group, she would not admit that she also had needs. She wanted to be important and show others that her life was all in order. She wanted to help others without opening her own life before God.

Suzanne is not too different than some of us. I had my own unresolved feelings to face during my groups, too. It was both embarrassing and humbling to admit I still had pockets of unresolved emotional pain. It was even more difficult to admit the times I didn't have the answers to the difficult problems presented.

When my unresolved pain was triggered, this is how I felt:
— "I don't want to admit I have needs."
— "I don't want to appear to need help."
— "I don't want to look at my own feelings."
— "I don't want NOT to have all the answers."

When we resist or deny our own feelings, the secret motive within our group shifts from helping others to protecting "me."

Here are some of the ways this happens.

1. **Manipulating:** When we need others to change so we look good or the purpose for them changing is to meet my needs.

    Manipulating selfishly validates our own self-worth by controlling others.

    > —*Secret Motive: If they do it my way, I must be right.*

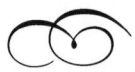

2. **Judging:** When we criticize others' efforts to change by bringing correction, criticism or condemnation upon their actions.

    Judging others' actions undermines their ability to hear and follow God.

    > —*Secret Motive: I want to keep control in their life so I do not feel inadequate.*

3. **Pride:** When we believe we have the solutions to their problems.

   Pride keeps us looking in a mirror instead of into someone's heart.

   —*Secret Motive: I want to have all the answers so I feel validated and important.*

1. **Compromise:** When we address the presenting symptoms or problem without looking at truth and root issues.

   Compromise of the truth tells people they can change their behavior without changing their heart. We fail to recognize their deep needs when offering circumstantial change.

   —*Secret Motive: I don't have a clue what's going on but I always have to have an answer.*

5. Rescuing: Relieving others of responsibility when they are capable but choose not to be.

Rescuing perpetuates immobilization by relieving someone of facing responsibility and/or consequences.

—*Secret Motive: I need to fix their pain so I don't have to look at mine.*

When our focus shifts from encouraging and loving to our own self-protection, we draw people away from God and pull their attention toward us. Isaiah 64:8 reminds us, "O Lord, You are our Father. We are the clay, You are the potter," (NIV). God chooses to mold us and make us into His image through many different methods. We cannot dictate or conclude just how He will do it.

We must be careful not to step into His shoes and play His role. Our job is to help others recognize where they have drifted away from God.

One of my old Webster pocket dictionaries says the word "facilitate" means to "make easy." I compare facilitating support groups to a set of windshield wipers. We don't drive the car, we cannot turn on the blinkers, we cannot press the brakes, but we can help clear the windshield for a clear path to avoid future accidents.

What are some of the ways we can be sure our motives for ministry are pure?

— **Admit your own needs.**

— **Confess your weaknesses.**

— **Risk looking at your own unresolved issues or feelings.**

— **Seek your value through Jesus.**

— **Ask someone to hold you accountable**.

Looking at our own lives and our continued need of a Savior is the best model we can be for someone. How can we convince someone of the need for Christ if we cannot admit our own?

Ask Papa God, "Do I have any secret or impure motive for wanting to begin a support group?" _____

If so, take your feelings and offer them to Jesus by following the five steps I just explained.

I admit my needs are

_____

I confess my weakness' are

_____

My real true feelings are

_____

Pray the following -

"Lord, I choose to seek my value through You by resting in the Truth of Your Word and meditating on Your promises.
I ask for Your forgiveness for previously seeking my value through

_____

_____

_____

I will ask (your accountability partner or leader) _____ to hold me accountable for today's confession and receiving Your forgiveness."

3

Getting Started

" . . . For the Lord will go before you, the God of Israel will be your rear guard. "

—Isaiah 52:12

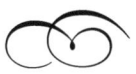

∽

A successful group will be the result of prayer and preparation. Without God's direction, the group has nothing to hold it together.

— **Purpose - What is the purpose for the group?**

— **Mission - Who will be reached through the group?**

— **Vision - What is the vision for ministry?**

How will accomplish the group's mission and vision?

Whether your group is to be structured or informal, laying down a foundation and establishing some guidelines will enable you to stay on task. This chapter highlights those considerations.

The Meeting Place

The place you select should comfortably seat the number of people expected and be private enough to foster intimate discussions. I like round robin type seating with all chairs facing into the circle, including my chair. Each week I sit in a different place in the circle to keep it fresh and in motion. This helps other's who tend to sit in the same place each week to sit by someone different and see the group from a different perspective. I usually only make available the amount of chairs to fit the group size so there aren't empty chairs. Oh, don't forget boxes of tissue!

Here are some suggested locations to check on, most of which will not charge you space rent. You could meet in a church classroom or office, a home (but not the leader's home), a community center classroom, a Christian school classroom, a business reception area (after hours), or a library. Some banks also have a community room available and occasionally a public school will consent to lending you a classroom.

Your meeting should be at the same location each week. Imagine showing up, the group has moved, and you were not notified! Ask the landlord for a commitment to use the premises for a specified term.

Interruptions such as telephones ringing and people knocking on doors can be quite distracting. If your location is such that interruptions are possible just hang a sign on the door reading

Do Not Disturb — Meeting In Progress

Unless the group involves children, ask parents to pre-arrange for childcare.

Format

How will you conduct the meetings? For instance, in addition to following the Dancing on the Graves of Your Past material, will you adapt the content or create your own agenda or offer counseling or other resources?

Our groups were always most effective when there was a balance of teaching, discussing, and praying.

1. Teaching:

Jesus said, "I am the light of the world. Whoever follows Me will never walk in darkness, but will have the light of life," (John 8:12, NIV). Teaching the truths in God's Word will correct inaccurate beliefs about God and how He feels about us, which is the root of most of our problems. The other half of our problems rests in inaccurate thinking about ourselves. So it is also important to teach the facts about overeating, homosexuality, abortion, sexual compulsion, divorce, etc. We are instructed in Romans 12:2 not to be conformed to the world, (its thinking or beliefs), but to be transformed by the renewing of our mind. Our teaching must reinforce the truth about who Jesus is and who we are in Him.

Teaching material will be from Dancing on the Graves of Your Past book and from your own experiences and education on the topics.

2. Discussing:

Opening the group for discussion allows you to hear how the members feel about themselves and God. How members interpret God, themselves, and the world around them will reveal where they need help.

3. Praying:

Groups grow when members not only receive but have opportunity to give. Prayer invites every member to become an ambassador of Jesus Christ by ministering His grace and love. Taking every question, conflict, and problem to the feet of Jesus accomplishes two things. First, it invites hearts to open and receive healing. Second, it takes the focus off of us and puts it directly on the Healer, Jesus.

Press in for healing at every opportunity someone is willing. These are usually Divine appointments to see God move. When people are emotionally healed there is a greater opportunity for physical healing. Our minds and bodies are the scenes of the crimes against us. Often we carry illnesses due to unresolved emotional distress.

Cross Talk

Traditional twelve-step groups like Alcoholics Anonymous do not allow members to "cross-talk." This typically means when someone is talking others refrain from dialogue or conversation unless using personal "I" statements. Not allowing two-party discussions does eliminate the group members from being confrontational or advice-giving, but it also limits the support and interaction needed to bring closure to presented problems.

I want each member of my group to be open enough to invite Jesus into every aspect of any problem without confrontation or criticism. We grow when problems are discussed and choices are presented. The group must work as a whole to accomplish this. Toward this end, here are a few group rules that can help discussions stay focused:

— **No gossip.**

Members are there to work on their own individual problems, not someone else's problems or symptoms.

— **No judging.**

Avoid comments that correct, condemn ot criticize.

— **No advice-giving.**

Do not preach or tell someone what should be done.

— **No interruptions or "quick fixing."**

Whether someone is talking, crying, or angry, allow that person the expression of that feeling.

Balance conversations by not analyzing or spiritualizing someone's problems. Feelings require a response, not an intellectual comment. It is the facilitator's job to stop inappropriate conversations and bring them to the group's attention. (See Guidelines for Support Groups in the Appendix Handout section.)

Open or Closed Groups

In an open group, members can come and go without continued commitment or accountability to the group or its facilitator. Open groups tend to be more oriented towards outreach, drawing members in by the "open arms" format. The group will see new faces and hear new issues that keep it moving.

The open group is limited, by nature of its purpose, in its level of intimacy. Trust takes time to build. Members may be unwilling to reveal hurts or feelings for fear of too much exposure to someone they may never see again in the group.

Closed groups invite intimacy and trust. This closeness offers a safe and protected environment in which to share feelings. For people who try to hide their feelings, a closed group could be threatening. The invitation to intimate communication can trigger trust issues and offers little place to hide emotions. Trust is a gradual process. The consistency of the facilitator and group commitment enables trusting relationships to build.

Screening Applicants

Not everyone who wants to be in a group may need your group! Screening applicants gives you an idea of how many to expect and to ensure everyone is coming for the right reason.

When I prescreen applicants, I am looking for answers to the following questions:

— **What do they expect from our group?**

— **Are they able to commit to the group and its purpose?**

— **Can they commit to the group's dates and times?**

— **Do they seem willing to look at their own issues?**

— **What can they contribute to the group as a whole?**

— **Is this where God wants them now?**

— **Do you, as the interviewer, have any "gut" feelings about this person that would cause you to decline them for attendance? TRUST WHAT YOU FEEL...This is discernment in action!**

You can contact them initially through email or snail mailing an application but I make a point to always have a one-on-one interview in person or by telephone.

I personally do not simply prescreen through a list of qualifying questions, but I am also seeking a variety and balance between their issues and experiences. I do not want my entire group to consist of women who just recently had repressed memories surface, for example. Neither do I want my group to be all women who have been working on their issues for twenty years. I find a balanced group of levels and issues works best in the support group setting.

After prescreening and praying either sign them up, place their name on a waiting list, or (if this is an option for you) bring them into individual counseling until they are ready for a group setting.

Mixed Gender Groups

Whether to mix male and female members in the same group will depend on the group's purpose and format. Both men and women share basic emotions like rejection, abandonment, fear, shame, and loss. But when sexual issues, such as incest, rape, sexual compulsion, homosexuality, or masturbation are being disclosed, separate groups for men and women should be considered.

After counseling men and women together in the first few groups, then separating them, we realized the mixed groups were hindered in their level of intimacy and emotional freedom. We also learned that discussion of sexual feelings could incite or promote sexual sin in those struggling with fantasy or sexual disorders.

In the beginning, we also allowed parents to bring their molested children with them to group. The result, again, was a limited group. This happened mainly because the group's purpose was not established and, in trying to be all things to all people, we were not doing anything!

I do not recommend relatives, siblings, or close friends to be in the same group, unless the group is specifically geared for families.

Age Restrictions

The needs of a nineteen year old are different from that of a fifty year old. A wide variety of ages in your group will obviously cause some to not relate to each other. This does not necessarily exclude age differences, but it means you will need to draw out commonalties of emotions and experiences that are more universal.

Note: if your group ministers to those eighteen years old or younger, check to see if you need parental notification or consent.

Confidentiality

Keeping the confidence of each member promotes trust and security. But in circumstances that you question or have difficulty in handling, you need the freedom to discuss your concerns with someone who has more experience than you. This helps you best meet the needs of your group and the individual, while you continue to learn.

There may be circumstances in which you are required by your state or church to disclose. Specifically, any abuse to a minor or the elderly should be reported, along with the threat of suicide or corporal harm. The next section called Group Forms discusses the use of the intake forms we use. Check with your church officials and your state's child protective agencies to see if you are a mandated or required reporter of abuse.

I would like to underscore the importance of this by sharing an alarming experience. A mother told me she suspected her daughter had been molested by the same man who molested her when she was young. We talked about it and Mom knew the authorities had to be notified. She seemed to understand the importance of protecting her daughter.

She agreed to make the call to Child Protective Services and report her suspicions. For the next several days, I tried unsuccessfully to contact the family. After two weeks, I followed up with a telephone call to the proper agency. The mother had **not** made a report. The agency checked sent an official to the home only to find the suspected molester left home alone with the child.

Agency investigations came to the conclusion the child had not been hurt. I found out, however, that I would have been held responsible if the child had been hurt in any way. It was nay duty to protect the child regardless of who may have promised or perhaps, actually did, file a report. By not following up and making the report, I was contributing to the child's abuse.

Requesting your group members to sign a "Waiver of Confidentiality," and "Liability Release" notifies them in advance if you are a mandated reporter and/or that you reserve the right to discuss their situation as necessary to best help them.

Waiver of Confidentiality:

The undersigned understands that his/her case may be shared with (your church name) staff and/or leadership. The purpose of the discussion is to allow the staff to pray together about your concerns and to help one another understand and serve you in the most effective manner.

In cases of the abuse of children or elderly, or corporal harm to another or yourself, we are legally bound by the state of (your state's name) to notify the proper authorities.

Date_____   Signature _____

If a person refuses to sign the waiver then I recommend NOT allowing him in your group.

**Waiver of Confidentiality and Release of Liability should be reviewed and approved by your church or advisors before using it..

Group Forms

All the forms you will need are in the Appendix section of this manual. You have the option of using the ones you feel most meet your needs. They are designed so you may fill in your ministry information and then make copies for your group's use.

Sample forms are included in Chapter entitled "Forms."

- **Healthy Support Groups**
- **Support Group Guidelines**
- **Welcome Letter to My Family**
- **Applicant Information Group Participation Acknowledgment**
- **Name and Telephone Exchange**

Note: This manual is protected under copyright laws. However, I am giving my permission here for you to copy the forms in the Appendix section for your personal groups' use only.

Advertising

You can provide a flyer or brochure announcing the group, where you meet, and who to contact. Most local newspapers offer a community section where they will print upcoming meetings and events. Advanced notice of several weeks is required, but it is usually very effective in reaching the community. Also local radio stations have a community bulletin board of on-air advertising of community events.

Place your advertisement on display boards at church and in your church bulletin. Send your brochures to other neighborhood churches to the attention of specific department heads. Also, Bible book stores often welcome announcements of this type. Ask the store manager if you can leave the information.

Email, phone, or snail-mail an invitation to those you think may be interested. Ask them to tell their friends, too.

Last but not least, arrange a kick-off seminar featuring key speakers, (like me!). The seminar can open the issues, address the need, and secure people's interest. Your group is a perfect follow up to such an outreach.

Advisors

Seek the counsel of someone you trust and ask that person to be a mentor for you and a consultant for your group. Another leader in your church could fill this role. Meet with your advisor on a weekly basis to talk about how you are doing and how the group is doing. As leaders, we must be accountable for our actions and what goes on behind our group's closed doors. Do not be a "Lone Ranger" at someone else's expense!

Resources

Assemble a list with names and addresses of outside people, agencies, and services. These referrals could be needed in an emergency or for additional support. Often your community has something already prepared and available for your use. Check with your local social services departments to see if they have a community resource list. Don't be concerned about a list that contains non-Christian help referrals…food and shelter is essential and any source is a good source.

Be sure your list includes resources from a variety of areas. For example, with regard to substance abuse, your resource list may contain private counselors, in-patient hospital services, out-patient therapy centers, Christian residential recovery homes, or on-going twelve-step groups.

If your group includes ministry to unwed, pregnant women, include information about pro-life choices, birthing classes, single parenting, residential facilities, financial assistance, adoption agencies, or attorneys.

A group that focuses on recovery from abuse may list crisis hotlines, battered women's shelters, co-dependent resources, and child abuse prevention agencies.

Included in your resource list can also be recommended books and tapes on your topic.

You may also begin a lending library. Everyone pools together their books and tapes on the topic or related issues. Others can check out the resources on loan. This is especially beneficial for people who are on a limited budget.

Fees and Costs

Most ministries are an outreach of a church and are supported by the tithes and offerings from that body. Other ministries are self-supported through donations. Charging a fee for group participation neither increases nor decreases your responsibility. Your legal liability as a mandated reporter of abuse wouldn't change, nor should your commitment to be fully accountable.

Besides advertising expenses, the actual cost of set-up is very minimal. You will need a room to meet in, your teaching material, access to a copy machine, drinking water, cups, and several boxes of Kleenex!

Note: Ministries that receive profits border on a business status and may Ml under government restrictions or be required to pay taxes. Check with your church or advisor as to their recommendations and guidelines.

Are you ready to bring all your group ideas and plans into focus?
Plan your group by using the
Organization Worksheet in the Appendix section.

4

Week One
"Welcome"

". . . For the Lord will go before you, the God of Israel will be your rear guard."

—Isaiah 52:12

The result of all your planning, preparing, and praying (and no doubt some panicking as well!) now sits before you, a group of anxious, needy people anticipating answers and direction for their lives.

This chapter begins a sample ten-week group. To help you stay focused I have provided an outline you can use in conjunction with planning each session of a 10-week group.

Weekly Outline

Week # _____

How to

   a. Teaching

- based on Dancing on the Graves of Your Past book

   b. Discussing

- based on homework from Dancing on the Graves of Your Past workbook

   c. Praying

- following examples in workbook or based on your inner healing training

Helps

- for leader and/or group

Homework

- supplemental ideas

Handouts

- optional information

A sample form entitled Week # is in the Appendix so you can easily follow this pattern when preparing for your weekly groups. Your outline will help you remain focused during each group session.

How To

As participants arrive, personally greet them and facilitate informal introductions.

Give each person a name tag and a folder containing the forms you want to use. (See Appendix for sample forms: Welcome Letter, Intake Card, Group Participation Acknowledgment Form, Letter to My Family, Group Guidelines, and Telephone Exchange.)

Note: Some leaders prefer to mail the forms in advance and collect them at the start of the group. If you choose to handle it this way, be sure you have extra forms for the members to fill out again any forms they forgot to bring, especially the waivers!

Read the Welcome Letter and then begin filling out the forms. After these are collected, circulate the Telephone Exchange Sheet. This is optional for anyone who wants to participate. There will be some people who do not want to participate. That is ok, there is no pressure. Those who do want to be available for prayer can fill out their contact information. Encourage them to call on each other for prayer since you may not always be available.

Discuss and review Healthy Support Groups handout and Support Group Guidelines (forms in Appendix.)

Call the meeting to order with words of welcome and prayer.

Sample Prayer...

"God, we thank You for the privilege of coming into Your presence through Jesus Christ. While we have just met, Your Word tells us You knew us from the foundation of the world. You saw our unformed substance, called us by name, and even know the number of hairs on our head. We couldn't possibly begin to know one another like You know us. You are aware of every need, every hurt, and every desire. We invite You to be our minister and group leader. Open our hearts and unlock the doors of fear. We ask You to fill our lives with the presence and power of Your Holy Spirit. We submit this group and our lives to You. Thank You for sending Jesus to be our Advocate, our Savior, our Provider, and our Healer. In Jesus' name we pray."

Teaching

By now a fair amount of time has already passed just taking care of preliminary business. The first week's teaching should be focused on the group and its purpose, personal connection and initial sharing why people are there.

Share your goals and objectives for the group, and, most importantly, share why YOU are there. Your testimony and call to serve will begin the bonding and building of trust process. Your attitude and style will carry over to the others watching you. You must model (by actions and expressions) what you want from the participants. Talk from your heart and others will feel they can too.

Discussing

After you share, ask the members individually to share why they is there and on what they would like to work. Begin with your co-leader if you have one, and then keep the baton passing. Remember, especially if you have prescreened applicants, you may know more about each participant than they know about each other. Talking with you one-on-one is much different than in front of new faces.

Ask for volunteers to begin. Some participants will need to be encouraged to share while some you will need to stop from sharing too much. A good way to monitor each story is to announce before beginning that each person has a specific amount of time to talk. However, most people will follow your example of sharing.

Praying

After everyone has finished and you are ready to wrap up discussion time, lift each name and circumstance up in prayer. Ask then first for permission to touch them. If it is ok, put your hand on each shoulder and ask God to meet their specific need and ask that the group will serve as His arms and ears extended to them.

Helps

- **Affirm the difficulty of sharing. (Thank you for sharing about . . , I know it was hard for you.)**

- **Ask questions if what someone says is unclear or easily misunderstood. (Did you say it was your father or mother that did ...?)**

- **Assess when what someone says triggers feelings in others. (Sue, you started crying when Mary said . . . .)**

- Accept when your own feelings are triggered. (I feel that way at times, too.)

Homework

- Read Chapter 1 in Dancing on the Graves of Your Past book
- Complete Chapter 1 in Dancing on the Graves of Your Past workbook

Optional Homework

- During a daily devotional time, read Psalm 51:6-12. Ask God to reveal the "truth" about yourself, Papa God and the Holy Spirit.

- Begin a journal, expressing your feelings to God. Share your secret fears, anger, and dreams as openly as possible. Try to pour out your heart in this intimate time with God. Write daily in your journal. If journaling seems like an awesome task, try following these examples:

a. How do I feel today?

   (I feel so afraid and lonely.)

b. When was the first time I ever felt like this?

   (I used to feel this way when Mom and Dad were gone and I had no one to talk to.)

c. How do these feelings, which are usually attached to memories, still affect me and my relationships?

> (Sometimes I still become angry at my parents when I call and there is never time to talk to me. I wonder if You, Lord, will always be there?)

> *A note about journaling. I recommend journaling that will initiate conversation with the Holy Spirit. You do this by concluding the journal exercise by waiting for the ministry of the Holy Spirit. Write down anything you feel is coming from God. We can be counseled, comforted or convicted with just a few precious words from the Lord. Maybe He will remind you of a scripture or give you a personal confirmation of His love. When I look back through my journal, I am reminded of how God saw me through each problem and doubt I had. My encouragement comes from His words of faithfulness in the midst of my trial.*

Handouts

- Pass out your Resource List (described in Chapter 4).
- Educate your group. It can be helpful to provide supplemental information around topics your group needs to grow in. Internet search and print articles, commentaries, news, interests, and Biblical examples or stories. Topics could include:
    - **Boundaries**
    - **Domestic Violence**
    - **Addiction Cycles**
    - **Divorce Recovery**
    - **Child Sexual Abuse**
    - **Co-dependency**
    - **Journaling**
    - **Listening to the Holy Spirit**
    - **Scripture verses on topic issues**

In **closing the meeting**, thank everyone for coming and acknowledge their contribution to the group. Emphasize that God is creative and will meet them at their individual point of need. There is no value to comparing their growth with others in the group.

Remind them of the next date and time you will meet and homework assignments.

Leader's Homework: Each week ask Papa God to show you what each person is struggling with (not always the obvious to everyone else), their value and contribution to the group, and thank Him for their growth.

Always be in prayer for the upcoming meeting, review homework assignment and prepare your outline.

Connect with your leader or mentor and let them know how you and the group are doing.

5

Week Two
"The Past"

". . . For the Lord will go before you, the God of Israel will be your rear guard."

—Isaiah 52:12

How To

Call the meeting to order with words of welcome and prayer.

"Lord, You know the heart of each one here and nothing has ever been hidden from You. You created us and know everything that has ever happened to us. Encourage us tonight to talk about the truth You are bringing us to face. We all desire healing and freedom. We no longer want to be stuck in an emotional prison. Educate us through Your wisdom and bring understanding to our minds. Help those who have never shared their story to be comforted. Help us to be good listeners. We invite You to be our counselor and minister. In Jesus' name we pray, amen."

Teaching

Dancing on the Graves of Your Past book

Book Chapter 1

The Past

"He brought them out of darkness and the deepest gloom and broke away their chains."
—Psalm 107:14

God partnered with us in our past when He gave us Jesus who died on the Cross and shed His Blood. Jesus took our sins and spiritual death upon Himself and through a Divine exchange, gave us complete amnesty and freedom.

When we accept Jesus' death in exchange for ours, His Cross becomes the grave site where our sin (including mistakes and bad choices) and old nature are atoned for, dead and buried, never more to be counted against us.

Then Jesus resurrected from the dead and returned to His Father in Heaven creating a bridge of reconciliation uniting Heaven and earth. Jesus now becomes the model we follow. He was a man in right relationship with God. We now have both the authority and power to be "the sons of God"… and daughters, too!

Seated with Him in Heavenly places with full access to the Kingdom's benefits, we have freedom from emotional distress, physical sickness, and spiritual torment.

Paul, in Romans 8:38-39, writes, *"For I am convinced that neither death nor life, neither angels nor demons, neither the present nor the future, nor any powers, neither height nor depth, nor anything else in all creation, will be able to separate us from the love of God that is in Christ Jesus our Lord."* Paul mentions the present and the future, but he doesn't mention the past. The past can't separate you from God's love because He sent Jesus, His love incarnate, to redeem the past. But the past *can* separate you from the awareness of God's love.

Discussing

Experience the Journey Homework Review

Did they finish the homework?

How did they do with it…any trouble understanding the assignment?

After writing their story,

    Were there any patterns they recognized?

    What did they learn new?

Who would like to share?

Ask for volunteers to begin. Some participants will need to be encouraged to share while some you will need to stop from sharing too much. A good way to monitor each story is to set limits on length of time allotted to each story.

If no one steps up to share, the leader should take over by returning to the teaching, sharing their own story, or address difficulty of trust with people they don' know and affirm the benefit of contribution. Listen attentively to stories, making eye contact and affirming their effort.

Workbook Chapter 1

The Past

"He brought them out of darkness and the deepest gloom and broke away their chains."
—Psalm 107:14

Paul, in Romans 8:38-39, writes, "For I am convinced that neither death nor life, neither angels nor demons, neither the present nor the future, nor any powers, neither height nor depth, nor anything else in all creation, will be able to separate us from the love of God that is in Christ Jesus our Lord." Paul mentions the present and the future, but he doesn't mention the past. The past can't separate you from God's love because He sent Jesus, His love incarnate, to redeem the past. But the past can separate you from the awareness of God's love.

What is your story?

Dancing on the Graves of Your Past ~ Support Group Leader's Guide

God partnered with us in our past when He gave us Jesus who died on the Cross and shed His Blood. Jesus took our sins and spiritual death upon Himself and through a Divine exchange, gave us complete amnesty and freedom.

When we accept Jesus' death in exchange for ours, His Cross becomes the grave site where our sin (including mistakes and bad choices) and old nature are atoned for, dead and buried, never more to be counted against us.

Then Jesus resurrected from the dead and returned to His Father in Heaven creating a bridge of reconciliation uniting Heaven and earth. Jesus now becomes the model we follow. He was a man in right relationship with God. We now have both the authority and power to be "the sons of God"... and daughters, too!

Seated with Him in Heavenly places with full access to the Kingdom's benefits, we have freedom from emotional distress, physical sickness, and spiritual torment.

God partnered with us in our past so we could now partner with Him in our future. God did it for love. He did it to destroy the works of the devil. He did it so we would be reconciled to Him. He did it so we would have a future and a hope.

If you have accepted God's gift of Jesus, it means you have accepted Jesus death on the Cross as redemption for all your sins and mistakes. It also means you have been given eternity in Heaven AND life abundant here on Earth.

Write out your experience of accepting Jesus as Savior.

Write out your experience with receiving the infilling of the Holy Spirit?

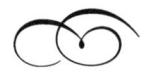

Praying

Prayer ministry should be comforting and affirming. Do not try to fix or control feelings.

Be aware of the spiritual atmosphere during and after all times of sharing. Trauma, fear, insecurity, shame, and so forth, can invade the room and bring heaviness. If this happens, bring it to the group's attention, and ask if anyone feels the heaviness in the room…..This teaches and validates discernment

Show them how to change the atmosphere by giving to Papa God whatever they are feeling, sensing, or seeing. Lead your group to focusing their attention on Him.

"Ok, let's give this to Papa God…" Ask them to hand to Papa God any of the heavy things they are sensing.

You model the prayer by YOU lifting it up to Papa God.

After they have done this, ask Papa God what He has for them in exchange…"Papa God, what do you have for me in exchange?"

Ask a few people to share what they received in exchange. You share, also, what you received. Encourage that God is good and close in prayer with hope and healing.

Important: The reason (in the workbook homework for this chapter) that I have them share their salvation and Holy Spirit experiences AFTER writing their stories is so that they are

NOT left in the midst of the pain and fear. Our goal is to bring them in touch but NOT leave them there or leave them vulnerable. I want them to be able to also capture their good experience with HIM.

Helps

Repeat the following "good listening skills" after people share.

- Affirm the difficulty of sharing. (Thank you for sharing about .., I know it must have been hard for you.)

- Ask questions if what someone says is unclear or easily misunderstood. (Did you say it was your father or mother that did ...?)

- Assess when what someone says triggers feelings in others. (Sue, you started crying when Mary said . . . .how did that make you feel?)

- Accept when your own feelings are triggered. (I feel that way at times, too.)

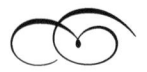

Homework

- Read Chapter 2 in Dancing on the Graves of Your Past book
- Complete Chapter 2 in Dancing on the Graves of Your Past workbook

Optional Homework

- During a daily devotional time, read Psalm 51:6-12. Ask God to reveal the "truth" about your self, Papa God and the Holy Spirit.
- Begin a journal, expressing your feelings to God. There are Journaling Exercise examples in the Appendix Handout section.
    - Share your secret fears, anger, and dreams as openly as possible. Try to pour out your heart in this intimate time with God. Write daily in your journal. If journaling seems like an awesome task, try following these examples:
        a. How do I feel today?

           (I feel so afraid and lonely.)

        b. When was the first time I ever felt like this?

(I used to feel this way when Mom and Dad were gone and I had no one to talk to.)

c. How do these feelings, which are usually attached to memories, still affect me and my relationships?

(Sometimes I still become angry at my parents when I call and there is never time to talk to me. I wonder if You, Lord, will always be there?)

When you are finished with journaling exercises always wait for the ministry of the Holy Spirit. Write down anything you feel is coming from God. We can be counseled, comforted or convicted with just a few precious words from the Lord. Maybe He will remind you of a scripture or give you a personal confirmation of His love. When I look back through my journal, I am reminded of how God saw me through each problem and doubt. My encouragement comes from His words of faithfulness in the midst of my trial.

Handouts

- Ephesian's Chapter 1 handout in Appendix.
- I AM handout in Appendix
- Pass out your Resource List (described in Chapter 4).
- Sample Journal Exercise A in Appendix.
- Educate your group. Do a few internet searches around topics your group has in common and print them for hand out.

Closing the sessions:

Thank everyone for coming and acknowledge their contribution to the group. Emphasize that God is creative and will meet them at their individual point of need, so there is no need to compare their growth with others in the group. Remind them of the next date and time you will meet.

6

Week Three
"The Invitation"

"But for you who revere my name, the sun of righteousness will rise with healing in its wings. And you will go out and leap like calves released from the stall. Then you will trample down the wicked; they will be ashes under the soles of your feet..."

—Malachi 4:2-3

How to

Call the meeting to order with words of welcome and prayer. Be sure to use eye contact and acknowledge them. Allow light conversation but start on time. This let's late arrivers know they are "late!"

Teaching

Dancing on the Graves of Your Past book

Book Chapter 2

The Invitation

"But for you who revere my name, the sun of righteousness will rise with healing in its wings. And you will go out and leap like calves released from the stall. Then you will trample down the wicked; they will be ashes under the soles of your feet..."

—Malachi 4:2-3

In the beginning I began writing letters to God, telling Him about what happened to me and telling Him how I felt. I vented and dumped all my emotions onto pieces of paper, recounting the abuse, rejection, and betrayal. I took hidden secrets out of my heart and placed them in front of God. This process brought me out of denial and led me to face the emotional pain that haunted me.

At that time I didn't realize from God's view my past was already forgiven and the door to the Kingdom already opened. These exercises of lamentations, graciously received by Him were, in fact, the beginning of my knowing Him. This is worth repeating…

At that time I didn't realize from God's view my past was already forgiven and the door to the Kingdom already opened. These exercises of lamentations, graciously received by Him were, in fact, the beginning of my knowing Him.

In *My Utmost for His Highest*, Oswald Chambers says that our knowing Him is like a man coming out of a dark cave into the brightness of His light. At first we can't see well, maybe even blinded by the brightness of the light, until our eyes get adjusted and we can see clearly. So it was for me. Jesus had already paid for the death and burial of my past—it was I who had to capture the revelation.

God began to slowly adjust my eyes to see Him more clearly and open my heart to accept His love. Healing came over the next three years—not all at once and not in a neat step-by-step fashion. Even though there were seasons that felt like a roller coaster ride, way up and then way down, at least I was strapped in the arms of Jesus and moving forward!

Guilt and shame, rejection and betrayal tried to sing the old familiar songs of my past to keep me focused on them. Release began when I could surrender it all to Him. The biggest breakthroughs came when I realized God was listening and responding to me! His responses weren't with thunder or audible words, but I experienced pictures, songs, scripture, and assurance He was with me, bringing comfort, peace, and joy! During these moments I felt wrapped in warm blankets of His love and acceptance creating a place of rest, peace and safety.

After a time, it was no longer important what I wrote to Him, but rather what He was saying and showing me.

I began to experience more days of joy and fewer days of torment. In the distance I could hear a new sound—a song accompanied by beautiful music. He had been courting me, coaxing me onto the Kingdom's dance floor with Him as my new partner.

Surrender and forgiveness were as at the core of my prayers to God, but those were merely my exercises of letting go. I also had to be willing to embrace a new belief system about God and my relationship with Him. I learned through my own experience and from others who I have counseled, what we believe about God directly affects trusting His love and living out our destiny in Him.

He is waiting to show you the mysteries of the Kingdom, just as He did with His disciples. He is desirous of an intimate relationship with you—to hold you close to Him, closer than any human embrace. God's availability isn't the barrier. The barrier is our misconception or mistrust of Him. Barriers are dissolved when we catch the revelation of who He is.

I know some things about the President of the United States. I know where he resides, what his duties are, and when he is on an overseas tour. But if I were asked about his personal thoughts or how to contact him in an emergency I wouldn't know. Even if I read his autobiography, I would have detailed information about him, but we would not be in relationship.

The same is true with God. Simply knowing about Him isn't enough. To assume we know God's will and desire for us without really knowing Him or His nature leaves us relying on our own faulty judgment and assumptions. Allowing past circumstances to be a guide for the future is like speeding down a steep road. What creates a victim is not what has happens to us, but remaining stuck in a pattern of thinking, believing there are limited, or no, choices.

A "victim mentality" places a ceiling on options and choices. We actually exchange the truth for a lie, and stay trapped in a cycle of unsuccessful attempts to fix something broken using broken tools. Here are a few examples.

Cindy loved God and was active in her church until about a year ago when her teenage son was killed in an automobile accident. Deep down inside she believed God may have taken her son away as punishment for an abortion she had as a teenager.

Dale had been a Christian for many years but on occasion he purchased pornographic videos from an adult bookstore. He would feel guilty and ask

God to heal him of his sexual struggle. After losing numerous battles with temptation, Dale believed even God couldn't, or wouldn't, help him.

A married Christian man was suspected of committing a morally degrading crime and held in a local jail. The accusation and humiliation were more than he could bear. After a few hours, the initial investigation proved his innocence but when the guards went to release him, they found he had hung himself with his belt.

Israel made a similar mistake in believing the Lord had led them into despair. They asked, "Why is the Lord bringing us to this land only to let us fall by the sword?" (Num. 14:3). Over and over they thought that bad circumstances amounted to fatal situations.

Peter, after Jesus' crucifixion, was confronted about his association with Jesus and lied (Matt. 26:69,70). In the midst of confusion and uncertainty Peter couldn't hang onto what he had known to be true about Jesus or Jesus' teachings. Overcome by fear and doubt, Peter moved into unbelief based on his circumstances.

After Jesus' burial in the tomb Mary's heart was broken believing Jesus was gone. Grief stricken over Jesus' death, she was weeping at the tomb's entrance. Mary, focused on her grief, was unaware Jesus was behind her until He called her by name (John 20:15).

These examples teach us three valuable principles.

- As long as we can trust the Lord and wait on Him, there is opportunity to see His ability to rescue and redeem us.
- Losing the ability to make choices removes hope.
- Choosing a desperate course of action often results in unfortunate experiences.

Until we learn differently, we can make the mistake of believing God is like a person we know—someone who failed to love, nourish, or accept; or someone who failed to love enough to correct and confront.

God's desire for you is greater then you can imagine or think. *"...no mind has conceived what God has prepared for those who love Him"* (1Cor.2:9). God has prepared things for us that are beyond our imagination and exceed our mental capacity. Our minds are a great creation of God, but our mind can hinder and limit our receptivity to experience the greatness of the Kingdom. We were meant to be ruled by our spirit, in-filled with His Holy Spirit. Filled with unbelief, doubt and fear, we journey through the maze of our minds to find answers, rather than into His Presence.

Jesus said if I was born again, I would be able to *see* the Kingdom (John 3:3). Jesus is talking about a revelatory experience here and now. The Kingdom is available to us, but we have to put on our "son" glasses to access it. God wants you to have full access to the benefits Jesus died for—that includes you getting your full Kingdom inheritance, the "life more abundantly" talked about in John 10:10.

My pastor, Bill Johnson, says what you think you know will hold you back from what you need to know unless you remain a novice. The biggest challenge we face is to remain open to *"all things are possible with God"* (Matt: 19:26).

Your false beliefs about God are corrected in intimate relationship with Him, allowing the ceiling of limitation and expectation to be replaced with anticipation and expectancy.

Making a choice to partner with God in your destiny is walking in identification with Jesus, rather than identification with your current circumstances, what has happened to you or the mistakes you made. What happens around you or to you isn't who you are and it doesn't define who you are called to be.

Lies we believe create the battles we fight. Fear creates a lifestyle that encircles around the lies and doesn't confront the truth until you face it. Hurt causes you to close your heart. The same wall that holds out pain also holds out love. When you choose to love it pushes you past the pain.

Mary tuned away from the grave site where grief and loss consumed her and turned to face Jesus. We must turn away from whatever is keeping us from looking at Him. This means we have to identify and acknowledge the things we have been giving our attention to, the things we have been clinging and holding onto—the dances we danced when we were hurting.

The King of Kings, Jesus, is inviting you to dance with Him in the Kingdom. If we will dance with Him, He will enter our pain and lead us out. The invitation set before us is to turn our attention and focus toward Him.

Discussing

Experience the Journey Homework Review

Did they finish the homework?

How did they do with it?

Any trouble completing the assignment?

Workbook Chapter 2

The Invitation

"But for you who revere my name, the sun of righteousness
will rise with healing in its wings. And you will go out
and leap like calves released from the stall.
Then you will trample down the wicked; they will be
ashes under the soles of your feet..."
—Malachi 4:2-3

In *My Utmost for His Highest*, Oswald Chambers says that our knowing Him is like a man coming out of a dark cave into the brightness of His light. At first we can't see well, maybe even blinded by the brightness of the light, until our eyes get adjusted and we can see clearly.

He is waiting to show you the mysteries of the Kingdom, just as He did with His disciples. God's availability isn't the barrier. The barrier is our misconception or mistrust of Him. Barriers are dissolved when we catch the revelation of who He is. What creates a victim is not what has happens to us, but remaining stuck in a pattern of thinking, believing there are limited, or no, choices.

A "victim mentality" places a ceiling on options and choices. We actually exchange the truth for a lie, and stay trapped in a cycle of unsuccessful attempts to fix something broken using broken tools.

Israel made a mistake in believing the Lord had led them into despair. They asked, "Why is the Lord bringing us to this land only to let us fall by the sword?" (Num. 14:3). Over and over they thought that bad circumstances amounted to fatal situations.

Peter, after Jesus' crucifixion, was confronted about his association with Jesus and lied (Matt. 26:69,70). In the midst of confusion and uncertainty Peter couldn't hang onto what he had known to be true about Jesus or Jesus' teachings. Overcome by fear and doubt, Peter moved into unbelief based on his circumstances.

After Jesus' burial in the tomb Mary's heart was broken believing Jesus was gone. Grief stricken over Jesus' death, she was weeping at the tomb's entrance. Mary, focused on her grief, was unaware Jesus was behind her until He called her by name (John 20:15).

These examples teach us three valuable principles.

- As long as we can trust the Lord and wait on Him, there is opportunity to see His ability to rescue and redeem us.
- Losing the ability to make choices removes hope.
- Choosing a desperate course of action often results in unfortunate experiences.

In what ways are you impatient or mistrusting that God can take care of you?

In what ways do you try to control your own destiny?

So, how's that working for you?

Until we learn differently, we can make the mistake of believing God is like a person we know—someone who failed to love, nourish, or accept; or someone who failed to love enough to correct and confront.

God's desire for you is greater then you can imagine or think. "…no mind has conceived what God has prepared for those who love Him" (1Cor.2:9). God has prepared things for us that are beyond our imagination and exceed our mental capacity. Our minds are a great creation of God, but our mind can hinder and limit our receptivity to experience the greatness of the Kingdom. We were meant to be ruled by our spirit, in-filled with His Holy Spirit. Filled with unbelief, doubt and fear, we journey through the maze of our minds to find answers, rather than into His Presence.

Jesus said if I was born again, I would be able to see the Kingdom (John 3:3). Jesus is talking about a revelatory experience here and now. The Kingdom is available to us, but we have to put on our "son" glasses to access it. God wants you to have full access to the benefits Jesus died for—that includes you getting your full Kingdom inheritance, the "life more abundantly" talked about in John 10:10.

My pastor, Bill Johnson, says what you think you know will hold you back from what you need to know unless you remain a novice. The biggest challenge we face is to remain open to "all things are possible with God" (Matt: 19:26).

Read the first chapter of Ephesians. This chapter is full of God's blessings to us who believe and a reminder of what a heritage we have in Jesus. What does it tell you?

Which declarations, provisions and promises in Ephesians 1 are you embracing and living in partnership with? Don't write "the right answers" or what you have been taught to be true. Be honest and let your heart speak to you.

_____
_____
_____
_____
_____
_____
_____
_____
_____
_____
_____
_____
_____
_____
_____
_____
_____
_____
_____
_____
_____

Which declarations provisions and promises in this same chapter are challenging for you to embrace or believe? Don't write "the right answers" or what you have been taught to be true. Be honest and let your heart speak to you.

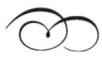

This next exercise is to help you take a closer look at a particular past issue.

- **First, reread your story from Chapter 1.**

- **Then pray...** *"Papa God...You know all the details of my life. Which event do you want to bring to my attention right now?"*

The prayer is asking Him to search your heart. In other words, you are asking Papa God from the story you wrote, which ones He wants to bring to the front to work on right now.

- **As soon as you finish the prayer, you will listen and then write out the first things He brings up. It may be something obvious or it may be something different that you originally overlooked.**

Ready...

Now pray, *"Papa God, You know all the details of my life. Which event do You want to bring to my attention right now?"* Write the first thing He shows you.

1. _____
   _____

Now again, *"Papa God, is there another event You want to bring to my attention right now?"* Write the first thing He shows you.

2. _____
   _____

Now again, *"Papa God, is there another event You want to bring to my attention right now?"* Write the first thing He shows you.

3. _____
   _____

Continue until you feel that is all there is for now.

4. _____
   _____

5. _____
   _____

6. _____
   _____

Look over the list you just accumulated and ask Papa to highlight just one situation to use through out the balance of the workbook. This will establish a format for you to use in the future. With that event in mind, answer the following questions.

- **How old were you at the time this occurred?**

    My example… "I was 9 years old"

    _____

- **What happened?**

    My example… "I witnessed my dad attack and attempt to rape my mom. My mom called for me to help and when I came into the room I saw my dad hitting my mom and attempt to rape her. He pulled at her clothes and was yelling at her. He was naked. When he saw me, he grabbed me and pushed me out of the room and I hit my head against the door. My mom screamed and I couldn't help. I don't remember how we got out of the house but I never saw my dad again for a long time.

    _____
    _____
    _____
    _____
    _____
    _____
    _____
    _____

- **What was your response to what happened?**

    My example…"I mostly felt afraid and worried if my dad would try to find out where we were. I thought he might break into our house and hurt us again. I didn't feel safe. When I went to school I felts ashamed about what had happened. I kept it all a secret and lied telling others that my dad died. I was glad we were away from him because I was afraid of him and didn't feel safe around him."

Dancing on the Graves of Your Past ~ Support Group Leader's Guide

Praying

For the balance of the weeks, center prayer time around those who did not apprehend the teaching or fully understand how to pray through the exercise.

Helps

This week it will be important that you "guide" stray stories and conversations. Refer to the section later in this guide about "Handling Difficult People."

- **Guide stray stories**

If everyone is disclosing their feelings and the next person begins to talk about their mother's surgery, stop and redirect the focus. Let each one know that stories need to be focused on first person experiences. You might say, "We can't talk about your mother's surgery in this group. Would you like to share about why you are here or how you are feeling about being in the group?"

- **Gather facts**

Sometimes due to emotional strain, nervousness, or memory loss, events are mixed up and not told in sequence. Never be afraid to ask a question if the story is hard to follow or if the events are unclear. Let them know you do not want to miss what they are saying.

Give permission to grieve

Grieving is the process of experiencing loss. It takes more strength to quietly sit and hold someone's hand while he cries than it does to fill he empty space with chatter, even if it is a prayer. Allow someone the expression of his feelings as long as it does not attempt to bring hurt to m or anyone in the group.

- **Grow with your group**

Do not be surprised if your own emotions are triggered by what you hear. If you stay open to your feelings, God can use the group to help you continue to grow. Your vulnerability, not your perfection, helps others to be real.

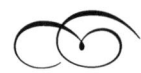

Homework

- **Read Chapter 3 in Dancing on the Graves of Your Past book**
- **Complete Chapter 3 in Dancing on the Graves of Your Past workbook**

Handouts

- Extra copy of "not-to-be-mailed" letter in Forms section if needed.
- Optional Journal Exercise B in Appendix.

7

Week Four

"Old Music"

"Come! Whoever is thirsty, let him come; and whoever wishes, let him take the free gift of the water of life."

— Revelations 22:19

How to

Call the meeting to order with words of welcome and prayer. By now some members are feeling comfortable and others are not sure! This is getting down to specific issues. Reinforce the benefit of reaching out to each other for prayer if needed.

Teaching

Dancing on the Graves of Your Past book

Book Chapter 3

Old Music

"The dead man came out, his hands and feet wrapped with strips of linen, and a cloth around his face. Jesus said to them, Take off the grave clothes and let him go."
—John 11:44

As a pastoral counselor I meet with people who are experiencing some variation of personal conflict resulting from spiritual, emotional, physical, and/or sexual issues. Unresolved conflicts became personal cancers that ate away at their hope and sabotaged their future.

Most of us are born with the belief we are safe. However, when abuse occurs, trust and safety is breached. Intrusion through trust and safety can be a traumatic emotional disturbance and continued emotional disruption.

Trauma is often experienced as a forced exposure interrupting and penetrating a safe environment.

Like the music playing in the background during a movie, the memories experienced with trauma and associated feelings create a backdrop from which life is lived and choices are made. The Old Music is the trumpeting of residual pain.

Post traumatic reactions may include anxiety, terror, guilt, blaming, detachment, agitation or irritability, restlessness, loss of interest in usual activities, loss of emotional control, grief, depression, uncertainty, thoughts of suicide, withdrawal from family or friends, communication changes, "startle" reflex, sleep disturbance, change in sexual interest or function, inability to be alone, self-harm, mistrust of environment or people, changes in appetite, and sometimes obsessive or addictive behavior.

While most people just want to forget what happened and move on, they can't stop the memories from resounding in the background. Sometimes the memories are loud and penetrating and other times can be quieted or ignored. Intense focus on silencing the memories from the trauma creates an attachment. The attachment involves such focus and interaction with the symptoms that the process resembles a type of interactive *dance*. The dance is a partnership. The trauma leads and the person follows.

The dance is in unison with the rhythm of the Old Music. Attempts to decrease, ignore, fight or deny the disabling symptoms associated with the trauma actually strengthen them. Fighting against the symptoms turns focus toward them and empowers their existence—the Old Music playing louder and louder until it is all that can be heard.

The relationship dance with the Old Music enhances the survivor's ability to stay connected with the past, allowing the memory to remain alive. Rehearsing and replaying the music are attempts to try to figure out if it really happened, why it happened, how they could have stopped it or done something different, or to find ways of revenge against their abuser.

Keeping alive the memory of the trauma allows the person to re-enter the scenario in an attempt to find resolve. It helps people who are hurting to prove the validity of what happened. The victim is often the only witness of the trauma who can testify to the trauma's reality. The symptoms are proof, to themselves and others, the trauma was real. They feel that without displaying their symptoms they won't be believed.

Someone may have accepted Christ as his or her Savior but still remains emotionally bonded to past trauma. His or her ears hear the truth that Jesus set them free but the awakened spiritual reality only accentuates the distance between the His truth and the Old Music. Feelings, emotions, and symptoms still attached to the Old Music are in direct conflict with the truth of God's Word.

It happens when we acknowledge the benefits of the Cross without really appropriating the Cross' benefits. The conflict surfaces because we never really allow (permit) the Cross to wash away the circumstances that draw the pain toward us. Because we hold onto our symptoms and are still in relationship with the Old Music, we respond when the memories are triggered and up they pop, painfully fresh and alive.

Sadly, we know the Old Music doesn't comfort us. It is just uncomfortably familiar, yet we keep the memory tight in our grasp. With the Old Music playing in the background, we dance the dance of guilt and shame, fear and blame, rehearsing the steps we know so well. We exchange the truth for a lie, submitting to the lie, allowing it to dominate and control us. The power of the Old Music is protected by our agreement and permission for it to remain in tact. The dance with the past is both unholy and ungodly.

Once we begin studying the Bible, we learn His Word is both a lens and a mirror. A lens magnifies the depth and revelatory mysteries of God. A mirror reflects back to us where we need to change our beliefs and mindsets in order to come into agreement and access His revelation. In other words, when we are confronted with the truth about God, we are also confronted with the truth about ourselves.

In the Psalms, David continually cries out and expresses his feelings, both happy and sad, to God. We, too, can express ourselves to Him. Feelings aren't right or wrong. They are a barometer that gauges our emotional state. One of God's gifts to us is the ability to laugh and feel joy as well as to cry and feel sadness. Our feelings are meant to work for us as an indicator of how we're doing. When our gauge begins signaling "alert... ouch... painful memory... shame... rejection" we sometimes put a pillow over the alarm.

Problems become intensified when we detach our feelings from events. This is called *denial*. Jesus was the master of confronting denial and bringing peoples issues to the surface. He didn't people please others and sometimes wasn't very nice! He stood in a posture as to allow the person to see their stuff and confronted in love.

In the story of the Samaritan woman in the Gospel of John (John 4:1-26), the Samaritan woman is going about her day and has not a clue what is about to happen. In the midst of her conversation with Jesus, He brings to the forefront her compromised past.

She has been married five times and was now living with another man. Jesus brought her emotionally painful situation right up front so she could be healed and set free. When Jesus finished talking with her, she was so happy she ran back to the village leaving her water pot behind. In confronting her pain, she was emotionally healed, filled with joy, and she left behind her old identity. She was the first evangelist in Samaria!

Sometimes a surface problem like a curtain conceals deeper, more significant issues. This happened to a woman attending a divorce recovery group. While discussing her failing marriage, she realized an even deeper struggle with rejection and betrayal from a childhood trauma involving her alcoholic father.

The benefits of allowing our past and pain to be atoned for through and buried at the Cross is in striking opposition to the consequences of burying it on our own through denial. The appropriation of the Cross, heals, cleanses and redeems. When we bury the pain on our own or try to forget about it, the volume of the Old Music may be low or muted, but it is very much alive. Because we are still in relationship with the Old Music, when the pain is triggered the emotions surface and the volume intensifies. The cycle gets reinforced, the symptoms are in control, and the Old Music has us captivated.

Why do the actions from who hurt you hold so much power over you? The Old Music has the ability to make us feel guilt or shame for what someone else did to us. I know it sounds silly, that someone would hurt you and you feel it is your fault. But it is possible to assume responsibility for the behaviors of others thereby agreeing with statements like, "It must have been my fault." Believing it was your fault is a type of false power—that you had the power to make someone behave a certain way.

You may discover that you are holding yourself responsible for the actions of others. Assuming responsibility for the sins of others can cause, what I call, "false guilt." No matter how hard you try, you cannot get rid of the guilt through repentance for these sins. They aren't yours.

Failed attempts to bring closure keep the bond to the trauma cycle turning, adding more steps of shame and guilt to the dance. False guilt is relieved when we come out of agreement and refuse to carry the responsibility for something God doesn't hold us accountable for. Our agreement with the lie that it is, or was, our responsibility or our fault keeps the memory empowered and the volume of the Old Music turned up loud.

If you experience unresolved shame and guilt, ask the Lord to show you, if in any way, you contributed to your painful experience. The answer may be yes, you did, or no, you didn't. Honesty with yourself is essential. What you believe to be true will expose the stronghold empowering the Old Music. Once the question of responsibility is answered, shame and guilt can be dealt with.

This seems like a simple thing to do, of course. But many people just aren't sure how to identify responsibility. Somewhere along the line, they believed—either through assumption or accusation—they were responsible for what someone said or did.

Ruth was molested by her brother. She told a friend who promptly said, "Well, my brother tried that stuff and I told him n*o*." Ruth felt guilty because

she didn't tell her brother to stop. She believed it was her fault he molested her. She rehearsed the memory over and over trying to figure out why she didn't tell her brother "*no*."

Bob frequently yelled and sometimes hit his wife when she failed to keep the house clean to his standards. His wife believed that if she could only do things better, Bob would be happy with her and stop getting angry. When the abuse continued, she blamed herself for failing to be a good wife.

Susan frequently took a shortcut home from school even though her parents insisted she take a safer, alternate route. With anguish in her voice, she told me it was her fault she was attacked and raped by two older boys because she did not follow her parents' instructions. Susan was consumed with guilt and shame.

In the 1980's when I told a pastor that I had been raped, he tipped his glasses, nodded his head, and said, "*Oh*." A few Sundays later his sermon included his opinion on how women "ask" to be raped. His position of authority increased my shame and guilt. Because he was a pastor and an authority figure to me, his words contributed to the lie I believed about myself.

To correctly answer the question of responsibility in these and our own situations, we need to have an understanding of abuse and its effects.

Here is a list of basic human needs:
- Survival (food, shelter, clothing)
- Safety (physical, emotional)
- Touching, skin contact
- Attention
- Mirroring and echoing
- Guidance
- Listening
- Participating
- Acceptance
- Opportunity to grieve losses and to grow
- Support
- Loyalty and trust
- Accomplishment
- Sexuality
- Enjoyment or fun
- Freedom
- Nurturing
- Unconditional love, including connection with God

Abuse is the exploitation or neglect of basic human needs. It can be defined as wrongful, unreasonable, or harmful treatment by word or deed. A child who is trapped in an abusive situation is like a prisoner of war with no power, no leverage, and no voice. Abuse has many faces.

Emotional Abuse

Words are powerful. The writer of Proverbs 15:4 says, *"The tongue that brings healing is a tree of life, but a deceitful tongue crushes the spirit."*

Emotional abuse demeans a person's character and dignity and assaults self-esteem. *"Sticks and stones may break my bones, but names will never hurt me"* just isn't true. A child's world can be built by words of encouragement and acceptance or destroyed by cruel, demeaning words. Neglect—the absence of words, time, or touch—leaves a child emotionally hungry, literally starved for attention.

With tears in his eyes, Robert told me his father had never hugged him or said the words, *"I love you."* Unfortunately, many children like Robert grow up never knowing if they are wanted or loved simply because they aren't told.

Types of emotional abuse include name calling, criticism, unrealistic expectations, absence of affection, not seeing the person's heart, not listening or affirming, belittling, blaming, and embarrassment.

Physical Abuse

Physical abuse results in bruises, black eyes, and broken bones; sometimes even death. Every blow causes damage to a person's dignity.

Punishing (inflicting harm through anger), rather than disciplining (training to bring about correction), is abusive treatment. The child is left confused, unable to understand the parent's action.

Physical abuse can range from withholding meals or other necessities of life to violent and unpredictable outbursts.

Women who admit being slapped or punched have said the humiliation and degradation out weighed the physical pain. The cycle of domestic violence affects children caught between two people they love. Children raised in physically abusive homes learn to inflict harm on others as a way to control people and situations.

Sexual Abuse

Sexual abuse among adults consists of any sexual activity against a person's will. It can involve viewing or touching for the purpose of sexual stimulation.

Sexual abuse of a child by an adult consists of sexual activity for the purpose of adult sexual stimulation.

Many children perpetuate sexual abuse toward other children as a result of his or her experience with being sexually abused. Sexual abuse of a child opens up sexual awareness much before God's intended time. Children are left confused and often unable to negotiate the effect of the interaction.

Children who have been sexually abused are damaged emotionally and often report feelings of worthlessness, betrayal, and helplessness. Sexually abused children tend to make poor choices regarding relationships and have trouble with intimacy, especially in marriage.

Types of sexual abuse can also include pornography, the exposing of sexual activity, lusting after someone, telling sexually explicit jokes, ridiculing parts of the body, misinforming about sexual function as well as violent and predatory behavior.

Randy was sexually abused by his uncle who was also his Sunday school teacher.

Questions and confusion about God are sometimes difficult to resolve when trust has been violated by an adult, such as a parent, uncle, teacher, or pastor, who held positions of spiritual authority.

Here are a few misconceptions about abuse.

Abuse Should Be Minimized

"I guess I should be grateful it wasn't worse. This has happened to lots of people." I hear that statement quite a bit from my counseling clients. In reality, abuse damages a person irrespective of duration, who the offender was, or the level of interaction. I like what Larry Crabb, a professional counselor and author, said during one of his seminars…*"The size of the gun doesn't determine if you have been shot."*

Abuse Heals with Time

"It has been five years. Why should I have to go through this again? I don't want to discuss it." However, time is not a healer—only a distancer from the pain.

Abuse Can Be Defined by the Act

"He never actually touched me, but I hated the way he looked at my body. I feel so stupid because I can't describe what he did." A person is abused when they are deprived of basic human needs or when their dignity is diminished or exploited.

It is unfair to the victim to imply a label be given to the event before feelings can be validated. The lack of validation or concern from others perpetuates the victim's need to hang onto the memory causing them to further express symptoms in an effort to be believed. But when pain is denied a type of emotional anorexia can develop to protect the victim from any feelings at all. Depression medications often suppress anxiety and stress but can also level out joy and creativity causing life to stagnate.

Secrets are sickness but openness is wholeness. Keeping a secret is very powerful. As long as the secret stays hidden, you hold onto a false sense of power that keeps you in control.

You may be wondering about the necessity to confront someone who hurt you. Confrontation isn't a prerequisite for healing. My father died before I was a Christian and began to deal with my pain. Therefore, I couldn't confront him directly. However, I could confront the truth.

Confrontation is about courage and love and the willingness to discuss conflict. But it should be done from a place of strength. Unless the offender recognizes and accepts his or her responsibility, you will set yourself up for more rejection and hurt. If you are still in danger of being hurt, you should refrain from that relationship until you and, hopefully, the offender can get some help.

Discussing

Experience the Journey Homework Review

Did they finish the homework?

How did they do with it…any trouble understanding the assignment?

What did they learn new?

What was the most difficult part of the homework?

Who would like to share?

Workbook Chapter 3

Old Music

"The dead man came out, his hands and feet wrapped with strips of linen, and a cloth around his face. Jesus said to them, Take off the grave clothes and let him go."

—John 11:44

Most of us are born with the belief we are safe. However, when abuse occurs, trust and safety is breached. Intrusion through trust and safety can be a traumatic emotional disturbance and continued emotional disruption. Trauma is often experienced as a forced exposure interrupting and penetrating a safe environment.

Transfer the information from the event you just identified and shorten the descriptions so they are brief and more concise or direct....

#1 Write a brief description of what happened.

My brief example of what happened..."I witnessed m dad's violent attack against my mom.

#2 Write a brief description of how you responded.

My brief example of how I responded..."I was afraid, didn't feel safe and I lied."

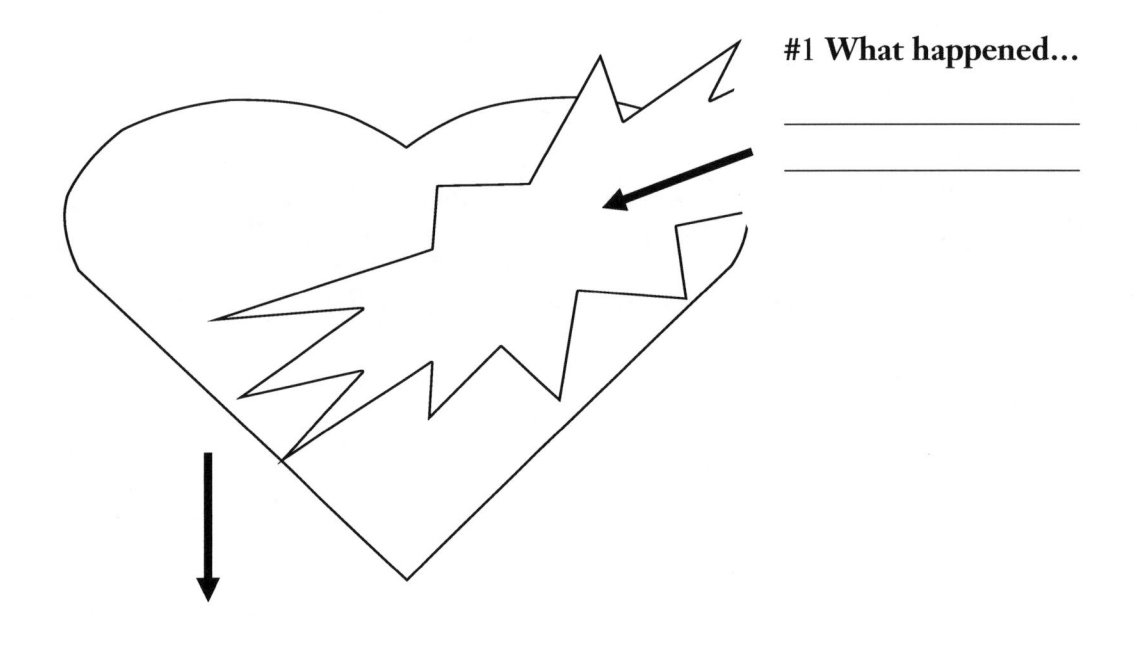

#1 What happened...
_____
_____

#2 How I responded...
_____
_____
_____

Like the music playing in the background during a movie, the memories experienced with trauma and associated feelings create a backdrop from which life is lived and choices are made. The Old Music is the trumpeting of residual pain.

Post traumatic reactions may include anxiety, terror, guilt, blaming, detachment, agitation or irritability, restlessness, loss of interest in usual activities, loss of emotional control, grief, depression, uncertainty, thoughts of suicide, withdrawal from family or friends, communication changes, "startle" reflex, sleep disturbance, change in sexual interest or function, inability to be alone, self-harm, mistrust of environment or people, changes in appetite, and sometimes obsessive, compulsive or addictive behavior.

Pray and ask Papa God to show you if there are left over symptoms from the painful event you identified in the last diagram. If He shows you something, use the arrows to describe the residual symptoms. Write down as many as He shows you.

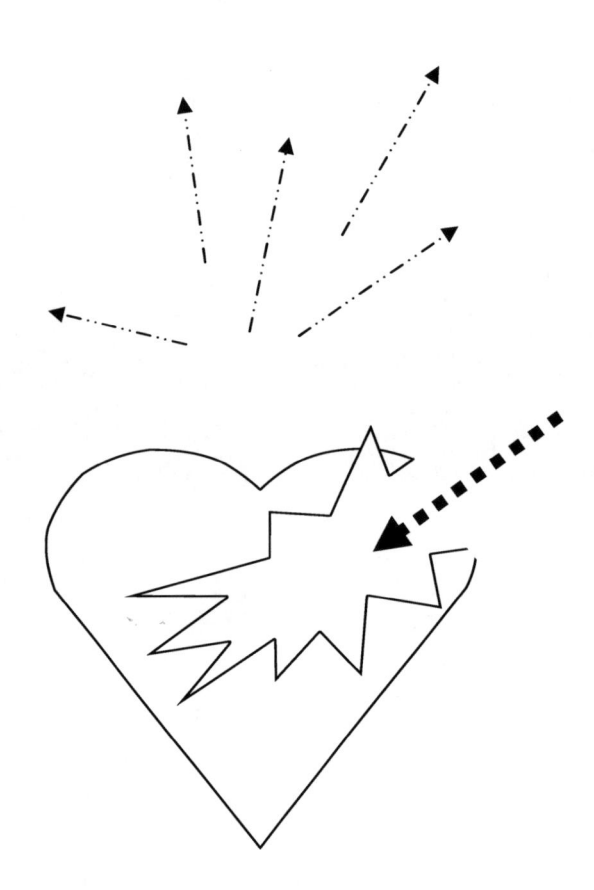

The relationship dance with the symptoms enhances the survivor's ability to stay connected with the past, allowing the memory to remain alive.

Rehearsing and replaying the music are attempts to try to understand:
- **Did it really happen?**
- **Why did it happen?**
- **How could I have stopped it?**
- **Could I have done something different?**
- **How can I get even with my abuser?**

Which of these do you relate to? _____

Keeping alive the memory of the trauma allows the person to re-enter the scenario in an attempt to find resolve. It helps people who are hurting to prove the validity of what happened. The victim is often the only witness of the trauma who can testify to the trauma's reality. The symptoms are proof, to themselves and others, the trauma was real. They feel that without displaying their symptoms they won't be believed.

With the Old Music playing in the background, we dance the dance of guilt and shame, fear and blame, rehearsing the steps we know so well. We exchange the truth for a lie, submitting to the lie, allowing it to dominate and control us. The power of the Old Music is protected by our agreement and permission for it to remain in tact. The dance with the past is both unholy and ungodly.

Abuse is the exploitation or neglect of basic human needs. It can be defined as wrongful, unreasonable, or harmful treatment by word or deed. A child who is trapped in an abusive situation is like a prisoner of war with no power, no leverage, and no voice. Abuse has many faces.

Here is a list of basic human needs:

- Survival (food, shelter, clothing)
- Safety (physical, emotional)
- Touching, skin contact
- Attention
- Mirroring and echoing
- Guidance
- Listening
- Participating
- Acceptance
- Opportunity to grieve losses and to grow
- Support
- Loyalty and trust
- Accomplishment
- Sexuality
- Enjoyment or fun
- Freedom
- Nurturing
- Unconditional love, including connection with God

Identify the needs you felt deprived of by placing a check next to the unmet need. How many needs were unmet? _____

Regarding misconceptions about abuse...

Abuse Should Be Minimized

"I guess I should be grateful it wasn't worse. This has happened to lots of people."

Have you minimized what happened to you?

_____
_____
_____

Abuse Heals with Time

"It has been five years. Why should I have to go through this again? I don't want to discuss it."

Have you felt time or distance from the pain is healing?

_____
_____
_____

Abuse Can Be Defined by the Act

"He never actually touched me, but I hated the way he looked at my body. I feel so stupid because I can't describe what he did."

Do you have a difficult time putting words to what happened?

_____
_____
_____

Why do the actions from who hurt you hold so much power over you? The Old Music has the ability to make us feel guilt or shame for what someone else did to us. I know it sounds silly, that someone would hurt you and you feel it is your fault. But it is possible to assume responsibility for the behaviors of others thereby agreeing with statements like, "It must have been my fault." Believing it was your fault is a type of false power—that you had the power to make someone behave a certain way.

You may discover that you are holding yourself responsible for the actions of others. Assuming responsibility for the sins of others can cause, what I call, "false guilt." No matter how hard you try, you cannot get rid of the guilt through repentance for these sins. They aren't yours.

Are you experiencing unresolved shame and guilt about what happened to you? Pray and ask Papa God if you have any responsibility or contribution toward your painful situation. Honesty with yourself is essential. Our agreement with the lie that it is, or was, our responsibility or our fault keeps the memory empowered. What you believe to be true will expose the stronghold empowering the Old Music. Write what He shows you.

"Papa God, show me if there is any part of this event that I am responsible for?"

_____
_____
_____
_____
_____
_____
_____
_____

Now ask Papa God, *"Show me which events I am NOT responsible for?"*

"Papa who is responsible? Why are they responsible?"

Write their name and what they are responsible for.

_____
_____
_____
_____
_____
_____
_____

Secrets are sickness but openness is wholeness. Keeping a secret is very powerful. As long as the secret stays hidden, you hold onto a false sense of power that keeps you in control.

Have you been keeping any secrets? _____

Who are you protecting? _____

Write down what the Lord might be showing you about keeping secrets…

_____
_____
_____
_____
_____
_____
_____

Confrontation is about courage and love and the willingness to discuss conflict. But it should be done from a place of strength. Unless the offender recognizes and accepts his or her responsibility, you will set yourself up for more rejection and hurt. If you are still in danger of being hurt, you should refrain from that relationship until you and, hopefully, the offender can get some help.

Do you feel the need to confront the person who hurt you?

_____

If so, what will you say or do?

_____
_____

One way to engage safe confrontation is to write a letter to the person being as honest as possible. The writing exercise allows you the opportunity to express how you really feel without the vulnerability of an in-person meeting.

Another way is to write a "not-to-be-mailed" letter. This exercise helps you keep a safe distance from the person. It helps you confront what happened rather than the person directly, especially if the person has passed away, the letter can be to the Lord on their behalf.

Now, you are invited and encouraged to write each responsible person a "not-to-be-mailed" letter. Remember that a not-to-be-mailed letter is *not to be mailed!* The letter doesn't have to be proper, punctuated, or perfect. This is an exercise in acknowledgment of the truth and isn't meant to be judged or corrected.

Use the following format as a guideline, duplicating it for as many letters as you feel you need to write.

To _____   or   *To Papa, on behalf of* _____

This is what you did…

_____
_____
_____
_____

You hurt me when you…

_____
_____
_____
_____

This is how it made me feel…

_____
_____
_____
_____

You are responsible for…

_____
_____
_____
_____

Your Name _____   *Date* _____

Prayer

For each letter, read it out loud then break the lie that you were responsible and ask God to show you the truth. Sample prayer...

"Papa God, I acknowledge my pain and loss and bring it before You. I ask You to forgive me for believing the lie I was responsible for what happened. I give responsibility back to the one who IS responsible. I come out of agreement with carrying the sin of someone else and blaming myself for their actions and wrong doing. I break the lie that I am responsible and come out of agreement with false guilt or shame. Papa, would You show me the truth?"

Write down what He shows you.

Before closing, wait and listen for anything you feel God may be saying to you.

You can be assured what you feel or hear is from God when it lines up with what the Bible says. His impressions, songs, psalms, and words can bring true peace. This peace isn't an absence of conflict but the inner assurance that God cares for you.

Write down anything you hear from Papa God right now.

_____
_____
_____
_____
_____
_____
_____
_____
_____
_____
_____
_____
_____
_____
_____
_____
_____
_____

**Ask Papa God what to do with the "not-to-be-mailed" letter you wrote...
What did He tell you?**
_____

Praying

For the balance of the weeks, center prayer time around those who did not apprehend the teaching or fully understand how to pray through the exercise. Following the workbook examples, offer to pray for those who want more healing.

Helps

- Talk about confrontation.
- Talk about carrying offenses.
- Talk about mercy triumphs over judgment.

Homework

- Read Chapter 4 in Dancing on the Graves of Your Past book
- Complete Chapter 4 in Dancing on the Graves of Your Past workbook

Handouts

- Optional Acknowledging Old Dances Journal Exercise C in Appendix.

Do you have other information you would like to provide to your group?

- Boundaries
- Discernment
- Trust

8

Week Five

"Old Dances"

"Give, and it will be given to you. A good measure, pressed down, shaken together and running over, will be poured into your lap. For with the measure you use, it will be measured to you."
—Luke 6:38

How to

Call the meeting to order with words of welcome and prayer. This is a more difficult week since most have not taken into consideration their behavior, protective attitudes, or how they hurt others.

Teaching

Dancing on the Graves of Your Past book

Book Chapter 4

Old Dances

"Surely you desire truth in the inner parts; you teach me wisdom in the inmost place. Cleanse me with hyssop, and I will be clean; wash me, and I will be whiter than snow. Let me hear joy and gladness; let the bones you have crushed rejoice. Hide your face from my sins and blot out all my iniquity. Create in me a pure heart, O God, and renew a steadfast spirit within me. Do not cast me from your presence or take your Holy Spirit from me. Restore to me the joy of your salvation and grant me a willing spirit, to sustain me. "
—Psalm 51:6-12

Adam and Eve were created to rule in dominion. Yet, in the midst of their most perfect environment, Eve contemplated there could be something she was lacking. The voice of doubt serenaded her with lyrics that followed an enchanting melody. She embraced it as her own and through one encounter of agreement, she was dancing with the enemy, swaying to and fro, listening to lyrics that soothed her soul (Gen.1).

Once the truth was recognized the dance of deception ended but the dance of shame and guilt began. Adam and Eve tried to cover their wrong actions by hiding from God. Guilt and shame were the result of real actions and choices. Looking at their life from our vantage point, it is easy to trace the steps and recognize where they messed up then tried to cover it up.

Yes, Eve's enemy deceived her. However Eve became the victim of deception at the point of agreement with the lies of the enemy. The music of intrigue and deception orchestrated by the enemy quickly became a dance of shame and guilt. The Old Dances are the coping mechanisms we use to cover the shame and guilt from our actions and choices.

The Old Dances of guilt and shame are sustained by the lyrics, melodies, and chorus changes (Old Music) we knew by heart. The Old Dance chooses distance rather than relationship. Distance (fear and hiding) enables us to remain in control.

God sent Jesus to redeem us from the Old Dance of guilt and shame, messing up and covering up. We have the opportunity to rule in dominion through the power of the resurrected Jesus. This is the Dance of the Kingdom in the arms of the One who knows us best and loves us the most. Jesus' power of the Cross, His Blood, His Atonement, and His Resurrection made it possible.

Jesus didn't die *for* us, He died *as* us, so our sins would no longer be connected or attributed to us (2 Cor. 5:21). His Cross is where the funeral occurred. Our old nature, our sins, our mistakes and our bad choices are all accounted for and discharged at the Cross, the place of our atonement and thereby the grave site of all our sin. Paul does an excellent job of explaining this to us in Romans 6—the death of Christ wipes out, cancels, and obliterates the record of our old nature.

A grave is a burial place, a place of internment, a final resting place, or the end of something. Dead things are buried in graves. Necromancy is having a relationship with something that is dead. As gross as that sounds, it is what we do when we remain in relation with the past and allow the past to control our future.

It happens very subtly. The Old Music gets louder and louder until it has gained our full attention. And then, here we go, with picks and shovels, the pain resurrected and resuscitated. With deception revived, the Old Dance of coping is all too familiar. After all, we already know the steps. It is the same old lie that enticed Eve, lyrics rearranged to personally minister to our longing and need.

The more uncomfortable process of the Holy Spirit reveals our connection to the Old Dances, our hurtful actions and attitudes toward others. It is God's answer to our prayer from Psalm 51:6-12 to *"create in me a pure heart."*

As children, we often needed self-protection to survive deprivation, neglect, or violence. As adults, our learned ways of protection can become the walls that close us in and keep everyone else out. Walls of self-protection become the obstacles that block intimate relationships.

My friends, Norma and Steve, adopted a newborn girl, Natalie, who was seriously ill. As an infant, her illness required twenty-four hour care. Either mom or dad was with her at all times. After she had outgrown the medical problems, her parents were able to leave her with a reliable babysitter. However, it seemed the only way Natalie could cope with the absence of her parents was to hide in her bed, cover herself with blankets and go to sleep. Today, at ten years old, she still displays fear of being abandoned and is very uncooperative and sometimes rude toward others.

As a young toddler if Rick cried after being put to bed, one of his parents would come in his room and violently shake the bed. This method stopped Rick from crying but also paralyzed him with fear at the sudden impact of his body flying up and down on the shaking bed in a dark room. Rick grew up with a fear of speaking out and expressing his needs. Consequently, he has never been able to trust close relationships or move beyond superficial conversations.

Children learn methods to protect themselves when they feel insecure or threatened. Both Natalie and Rick are coping with childhood events (the Old Music) that weren't within their power to control. However, they both compensated with behaviors that sheltered their pain (Old Dances) to help them deal with life. They adopted methods of self-protection to keep them safe.

Self-protective patterns can become the broken glasses through which life is viewed. Adults living with residual pain (Old Music) and recurring coping patterns (Old Dances) become imprisoned. The patterns that once protected now keep us locked up and the adult heart flutters and fights against the bars for freedom, thus the dances are in full swing.

Adults who live their lives through a coping mechanism or from a defensive position repeat patterns in choices and select, by default, the same unfulfilling reactions. They choose and make future decisions based on underlying false beliefs. The coping behavior is a vehicle to keep the pain shielded, like a bandage covering an open wound.

Initially the bad events may have happened to you without your choice involved. If the belief of helplessness takes hold you may expect someone, or God, to do something *to* you, or *for* you, to make it right or fix it. "*I am powerless and things only happen to me."* This belief keeps you stuck and cripples the ability to take ownership of choices or take steps to change. Walls are often reinforced with self-pity. Self-pity strategically accesses guilt and shame through the pain of the Old Music.

In contrast there can be a sense of entitlement. Since all these bad things happened to me…*I am entitled to compensation, free counseling, unending attention from others. I am entitled to mistreat others, be angry, and take out my pain on you.*

Sonia is an adult woman with 4 children. Sonia's mother whines and manipulates Sonia to get her needs met. After Sonia complies, mom criticizes Sonia for every action not approved of. Sonia has been trapped in her mother's control since a young girl. Sonia is frustrated and angry, feeling she can never please her mom. She is filled with self-contempt; yet, Sonia never thought she had the ability or power to set boundaries and limits. Somehow, this would dishonor her mom. Sonia, on the other hand, is mean and abrupt with her husband and children. She doesn't see that she is taking out her pain and anger on the people she loves the most.

Feelings of rejection, betrayal, hatred, anger, unforgiveness, and ambivalence are natural responses to being hurt. But when we harbor and protect them, we often reshape them into weapons to hurt ourselves or someone else. The coping mechanism or protective attitude reveals itself through sinful behaviors, manipulation and compromised actions.

Reacting out of our pain causes us to sin against others and God. By justifying our sin, we excuse or deny the thoughts and behaviors that hurt others. We may say, *"This is just how I am,"* or *"I've always been like this, and that is just how it is."* Or *"You have no idea what I have been through."* Justifying our actions is an invitation and excuse to rebel. Finally, we discount true guilt, God's conviction for our sin, and deny Jesus' atoning work on the Cross.

When God begins the work of showing us our defenses and protective behaviors, He also identifies attitudes we were completely unaware we carried. The Holy Spirit, called the Comforter or Counselor (John 14), brings the truth and inward cleansing and the changing necessary *"to be conformed to the likeness of his Son"* (Rom. 8:29). God instructs us not to partner with darkness rather to let darkness be exposed (Eph 5:11). It is His love for us that drags what is in darkness into the light. Healing requires we remain humble and honest and allow the deep work when the Holy Spirit draws our attention to the underlying issues and the ways we have created unholy and ungodly bonding.

Sinful cycles pass down from generation to generation. (Look up Exodus 34:7 and Numbers 14:18.) We can experience God's forgiveness and restoration through Jesus by repenting (turning away from) and renouncing our sinful thoughts and behavior.

According to 2 Cor. 5:21, *"God made him who had no sin to be sin for us, so that in him we might become the righteousness of God."* And Psalm 112:2 gives us a promise that the generations of the upright—the righteous—will be blessed!

When we invite the work of the Holy Spirit, He brings us into all truth. The Old Music and Old Dances have no power, control, influence, or dominance when demolished and disempowered through Jesus. True peace comes from being cleansed by God's grace and forgiveness.

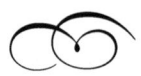

Discussing

Experience the Journey Homework Review

Did they finish the homework?

How did they do with it…any trouble understanding the assignment?

What are some of your own examples to share?

Who in the group would like to share?

Workbook Chapter 4

Old Dances

"Surely you desire truth in the inner parts; you teach me wisdom in the inmost place. Cleanse me with hyssop, and I will be clean; wash me, and I will be whiter than snow. Let me hear joy and gladness; let the bones you have crushed rejoice. Hide your face from my sins and blot out all my iniquity. Create in me a pure heart, O God, and renew a steadfast spirit within me. Do not cast me from your presence or take your Holy Spirit from me. Restore to me the joy of your salvation and grant me a willing spirit, to sustain me."

—Psalm 51:6-12

The Old Dances are the coping mechanisms we use to cover the shame and guilt from our actions and choices. The Old Dances of guilt and shame are sustained by the lyrics, melodies, and chorus changes (Old Music) we knew by heart. The Old Dance chooses distance rather than relationship. Distance (fear and hiding) enables us to remain in control.

Conflict is created when what we believe doesn't match up to what God tells us in His Word.

- I believe (God and my feelings/experiences agree)
- I want to believe (God and my feelings/experiences conflict)
- I don't believe (My feelings/experiences outweigh what He says)

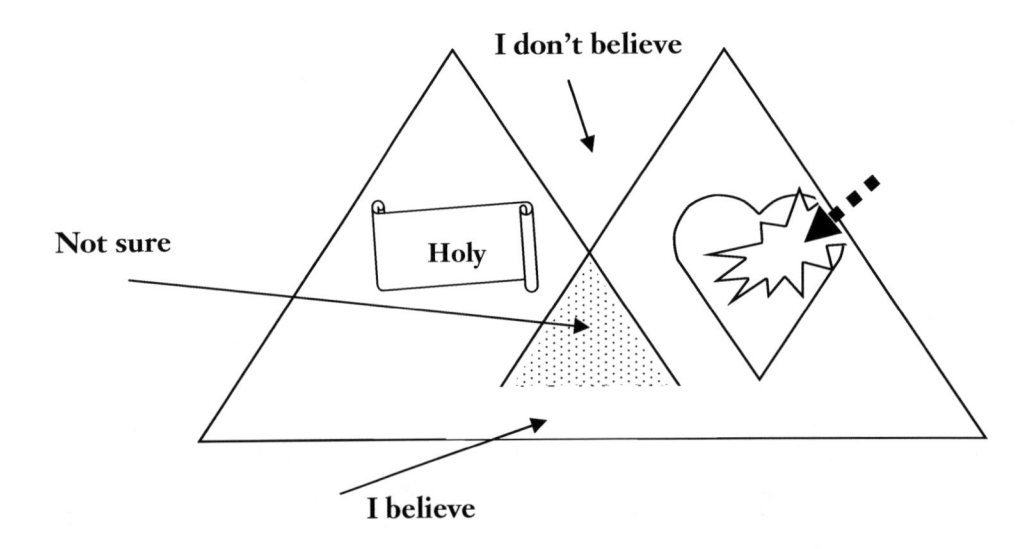

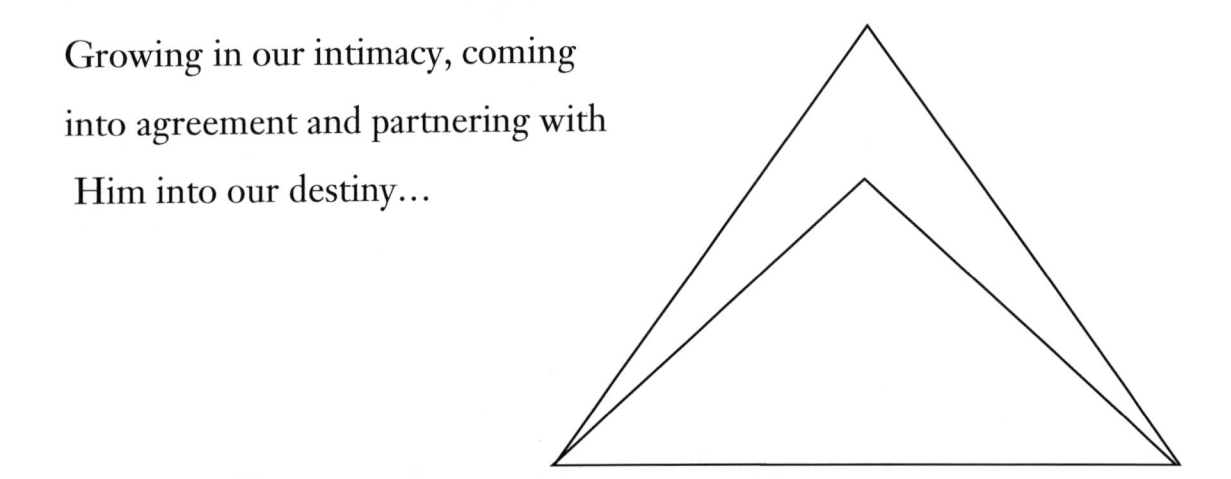

Growing in our intimacy, coming into agreement and partnering with Him into our destiny…

The more uncomfortable process of the Holy Spirit reveals our connection to the Old Dances, our hurtful actions and attitudes toward others. It is God's answer to our prayer from Psalm 51:6-12 to "create in me a pure heart."

Look up Psalm 51 and read verses 6-12.

As children, we often needed self-protection to survive deprivation, neglect, or violence. As adults, our learned ways of protection can become the walls that close us in and keep everyone else out. Walls of self-protection become the obstacles that block intimate relationships.

Self-protective patterns can become the broken glasses through which life is viewed. Adults living with residual pain (Old Music) and recurring coping patterns (Old Dances) become imprisoned. The patterns that once protected now keep us locked up and the adult heart flutters and fights against the bars for freedom, thus the dances are in full swing.

Adults who live their lives through a coping mechanism or from a defensive position repeat patterns in choices and select, by default, the same unfulfilling reactions. They choose and make future decisions based on underlying false beliefs. The coping behavior is a vehicle to keep the pain shielded, like a bandage covering an open wound.

Walls are often reinforced with self-pity. Self-pity strategically accesses guilt and shame through the pain of the Old Music.

Feelings of rejection, betrayal, hatred, anger, unforgiveness, and ambivalence are natural responses to being hurt. But when we harbor and protect them, we often reshape them into weapons to hurt ourselves or others.

The coping mechanism or protective attitude reveals itself through sinful behaviors, manipulation and compromised actions.

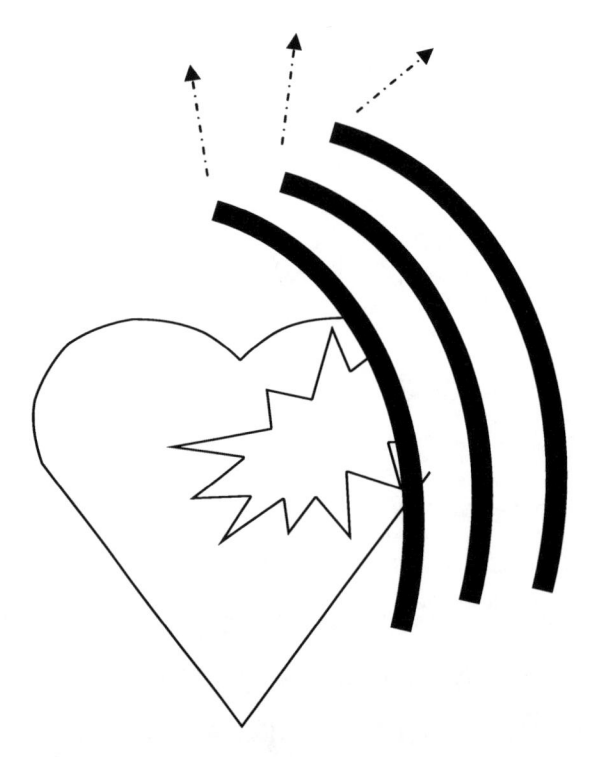

Ask the Lord to show you coping mechanisms you employ to keep yourself protected or to avoid dealing with painful issues.

1. _____
2. _____
3. _____

In contrast there can be a sense of entitlement. Since all these bad things happened to me…I am entitled to compensation, free counseling, unending attention from others. I am entitled to mistreat others, be angry, and take out my pain on you.

God instructs us not to partner with darkness rather to let darkness be exposed (Eph 5:11). It is His love for us that drags what is in darkness into the light. Healing requires we remain humble and honest and allow the deep work when the Holy Spirit draws our attention to the underlying issues and the ways we have created unholy and ungodly bonding.

How has your behavior hurt others?

_____
_____
_____
_____
_____
_____
_____
_____
_____
_____
_____
_____
_____
_____
_____

In what way do you justify or excuse your behavior toward others?

_____
_____
_____

Dancing on the Graves of Your Past ~ Support Group Leader's Guide

Sinful cycles pass down from generation to generation. Look up and read Exodus 34:7 and Numbers 14:18. Ask Papa God to show you which behaviors are generational and "learned" from your family or environment.

"Papa God, what behaviors do I demonstrate that are like my mother or her side of the family?"

_____
_____
_____
_____
_____
_____
_____

"Papa God, what behaviors do I demonstrate that are like my father or his side of the family?"

_____
_____
_____
_____
_____
_____
_____

According to 2 Cor. 5:21, "God made him who had no sin to be sin for us, so that in him we might become the righteousness of God." And Psalm 112:2 gives us a promise that the generations of the upright—the righteous—will be blessed!

Read Psalm 112:2 and pronounce a written blessing on your future generations.

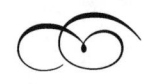

_____
_____
_____
_____

Praying

For the balance of the weeks, center prayer time around those who did not apprehend the teaching or fully understand how to pray through the exercise.

Helps

- **Remind the group that God knows everything and this is an opportunity to get rid of the baggage of pain AND the baggage of protective behavior.**

Homework

- **Read Chapter 5 in Dancing on the Graves of Your Past book**
- **Complete Chapter 5 in Dancing on the Graves of Your Past workbook**

Handouts

- **Promises I Can't Afford to Keep Journal Exercise D in Appendix**
- **Promises on Forgiveness are in Appendix.**

9

Week Six

"Dance of Surrender"

"Give, and it will be given to you. A good measure, pressed down, shaken together and running over, will be poured into your lap. For with the measure you use, it will be measured to you."

—Luke 6:38

How to

Call the meeting to order with words of welcome and prayer. This is the time to reassure your group that Jesus can walk into the pain and lead them out. The process of surrender opens the door to healing and release.

Teaching
Dancing on the Graves of Your Past book

Book Chapter 5

Dance of Surrender

I will both lie down in peace, and sleep, for you alone, O LORD, make me dwell in safety.
— Psalm 4:8

Jesus danced the Dance of Surrender so He and His Father would be "One." It was the beginning of Jesus following His Father's direction so in all ways He would be submitted to His Father. The Dance of Surrender is coming out of yourself and into God. It is about trusting Him—allowing Him to lead us into true freedom and peace.

As a child dances on the feet of their father so begins our Dance of Surrender. Our Heavenly Father knows our heart. He moves slowly and holds us close so we don't fall. Our first dance with Him beautifully demonstrates our "oneness" with Him as we move intimately together.

At the close of many church meetings, the preacher petitions the congregation with Jesus' invitation, *"'Come unto me, all you who are weary and burdened, and I will give you rest. Take my yoke upon you and learn from me, for I am gentle and humble in heart, and you will find rest for your souls'"* (Matt. 11:28, 29). The preacher then asks, *"Won't you come to the altar and give it to Jesus?"* The people march forward, pray a few moments, and go home to find they took "it" with them.

This reminds me of when my toddlers placed inedible and undesirable things in their mouths. We called it "yuck." I'd coax, *"Give mommy the yuck,"* requesting dirt, coins, bugs, or whatever, to be spit out of their mouth and into the palm of my hand. If the yuck came out, I'd applaud and praise with a sigh of relief. If the yuck had been swallowed no matter how much I coaxed or commanded, a voluntary spit wasn't going to expel the yuck. The only way the bad stuff was going to come out was by emptying the stomach.

Giving our problems to Jesus is similar. A simple word or two usually won't do it. It requires an emptying of self-will and self-protection. The "coming" must be accompanied with sincere motivation and desire to be rid of our "yuck." Resistance to surrender will drive us to the edge and limit of our own strength.

What does the Old Music and Old Dance offer that generates resistance to surrender? The answers are in the completion of the following statement;

If I keep this trauma-bond relationship in tact I won't have to feel, have an identity, face others, be responsible, be authentic, change, tell secrets, be honest, tell my truth, trust, be in reality, be positive, grow, be accountable, have relationships, be mature, risk, have goals, have values, be independent, have freedom, have in-

ternal validation, have a purpose, be connected with people or family, have dreams, have hopes, be successful, have faith, live, be in the present, obtain status, make decisions, have needs, have wants, have communication, intimacy with God or…(insert as it applies)

Resistance causes us to pray to relieve the symptoms rather than pray for revelation so there won't be symptoms. Sometimes it is easier to keep cleaning up the messes than to find out why we keep making them. Lasting change happens when we change our belief system rather than our behavior system.

The systems of the Old Music and Old Dance perpetuate fear of facing the future. Surrender is risk and willingness to face the future through faith and exercising trust through relationship with God.

The process can expose and trigger pain of vulnerability as that which we first experienced during the original trauma. Remember, when I was talking about trauma being a forced intrusion into a safe environment? The person in protective mode perceives themselves as now being safe. Protection is a disguise. Any intrusion into that artificially safe place is felt as penetrating and painful.

Alice was the youngest of three sisters, all of whom were molested by their stepfather. The problem today is that her mother is old and in poor health. Alice is going to visit her and wants to try to work things out, but there is something blocking her.

As a child, Alice believed her mother knew about the molestation and was not capable, or unable, to protect her so Alice made herself a secret promise. She made an internal vow she would never trust her mother again. Since that time and throughout Alice's adult years, Alice and her mom have never had more than a superficial connection. She knows she must let go of the vow of mistrust so she can forgive, heal, and make an attempt to build relationship with her mother.

Jessica was undisciplined and disruptive in her Sunday school class. The teacher was determined to take control of her class and Jessica! So with patience, kindness, goodness, and gentleness she gave Jessica lots of special attention.

Jessica was hugged, talked to, and finally the teacher pulled her up onto the teacher's lap. When the teacher reached to tickle her just above the knee, Jessica suddenly pushed the teacher's hand away and abruptly pulled her dress down over her knees. With a confident tone of voice, Jessica said, *"My uncle touched my private and he is in jail and I never have to see him again."* With that statement, Jessica jumped out of the teacher's lap and began her usual disruptive activities.

Jessica, at age five, had made a promise to herself that no one would control her again. As an adult, Jessica's commitment to that promise still holds her bound.

The dances of self-protection Alice and Jessica learned in childhood are affecting their relationships with others. Resistance to intimacy is fortified by promises we made to the Old Music and Old Dances. Today, if we want to grow in our relationships, we can no longer afford to keep these promises. Jesus wants our stability, security, and significance to be in Him.

The path to true happiness and peace is to love God with our whole heart, mind, soul, and strength.

David writes in Psalm 51:18, *"The sacrifices of God are a broken spirit; a broken and contrite heart, O God, you will not despise."* David responded so openly and truthfully after failing at his own strong-willed attempts to remedy his denial and deceitfulness. We may call Jesus our *Savior* but not allow him Lordship over our lives. Without surrender the Old Music and Old Dance have an open invitation for relationship with the lies that empower shame, guilt, and fear.

The Orphan Spirit

Thomas, in John, Chapter 14, was concerned after hearing Jesus' plans to go away. Thomas questioned Jesus and His promise He would not leave them, but would return to them. Jesus tells Thomas and the disciples *"I will not leave you as orphans…."* Jesus discerned Thomas' insecurity and fear. In recognition of Thomas attitude, Jesus identifies an "orphan" spirit manifested in Thomas' fear of being left alone, unprotected, uncovered, rejected and abandoned.

Jesus promised He wouldn't leave them as orphans but will send them the Holy Spirit called the Spirit of Truth (John 14:17) also translated in Greek as "The Comforter." Jesus also called the Holy Spirit "The Counselor" in John 14:26. In other words, Jesus was sending them Truth, Comfort, and Counsel in the form of the Holy Spirit. who would be both *with* and *inside* them.

The orphan spirit, in an attempt to hide pain and brokenness, seeks protection and cover up from allies. Three prominent allies are the *unloving spirit*, the *religious spirit* and the *punishing spirit*. If these barriers exist, they must be conquered so surrender will be pure and unhindered, or manipulated.

The Unloving Spirit

During a support group a young woman remained reserved and distant. We encouraged her to let God have her pain. *"I don't like to pray out loud,"* she said. We said we would join her in silent prayer. She refused. We encouraged her to tag along on our prayers. She refused. Perplexed and trying to build a bridge through her resistance, I offered her, once more, to allow us to pray for her. Now crying, she shook her head and firmly refused. She was unable to receive God's love and forgiveness.

The unloving spirit protects the orphaned heart by blocking the ability to give and receive love both from others and God. The melody plays in harmony with the Old Music, rooted in the past and its footsteps can be tracked throughout the Old Dances. Out of default, the unloving spirit will reject before it gets rejected—it will desire love but behave unlovely.

Love actually brings justice and requires protection. Those who are unable to give and receive love reject the work of the Cross and the Blood of Jesus and thereby reject the "love" God sent them.

The unloving spirit manipulates the orphan heart with unworthiness, pity, condemnation, and accusation. It judges, accuses, criticizes and manipulates. It will embrace the comfortably uncomfortable, rather than surrender to God's love.

Because the Old Music and Old Dance maneuver a perpetual state of need, longing for love, always on the brink of crisis, the orphaned heart ends up asking what more God could possibly want them to do. And that is their problem. God doesn't want them to do anything. He wants them to let Him do something! He wants them to allow His love and infilling so they experience love and can love others.

The invalid man by the pool of Bethesda in John's Gospel (John 5:8) had been a victim of his circumstance for so long that when Jesus asked him if he wanted to be well, he began rehearsing his problem. Jesus already knew the problem. All the man needed to do was to come out of focus on himself and come into focus on God.

Jesus then commanded the invalid to pick up his mat and walk. The man picked up his mat and walked. He was cured! Later, when Jesus found the man, he told him, *"... you are well again. Stop sinning or something worse may happen to you"* (John 5:14). The reference to the man's sin raised a question for me. What sin was Jesus referring to? Jesus' comment was caution against any temptation to live his life separated from love. Jesus was warning him not to follow after an unloving spirit. Now that Jesus had healed him, a greater dimension of relationship was expected. Jesus considered anything less than that to be a sin. Many people are camped out by their own pools of despair and Jesus' invitation to surrender will evoke excuses, an inability to receive love.

The Religious Spirit

The religious spirit covers the orphaned heart with performance and works. Completing a fifteen-week self-defense course, their lives in neat little packages, and along comes the "invitation" to give it all up! *"You must be kidding! I have worked very hard to get where I am and no one is going to take it from me again. Only the strong survive."*

The orphaned heart's pain is covered by masks of overeating, oversleeping, overworking, or addictions to pornography, alcohol, drugs, or self-injury. Sometimes the religious spirit is manifested in fear, hiding the orphan heart behind locks, security buildings, police dogs, whistles, or self-defense classes; maybe hiding behind anger, verbal abuse, assault, pride, procrastination and even hopelessness.

Consequently, the religious spirit is fixated on self-reliance and those things which they can control. Within the Old Music and Old Dance they have created a fortress and any uninvited intrusion reinforces the barriers.

Mark's Gospel story about a rich young man gives us another illustration. *"Jesus looked at him and loved him. ... 'Go, sell everything you have and give to the poor, and you will have treasure in heaven. Then come, follow me.' At this the man's face fell. He went away sad, because he had great wealth"* (Mark 10:21-23). Jesus' concern wasn't the man's wealth, but the man's heart, which placed wealth above his relationship with Jesus. Just like this rich man, the religious spirit will hang onto any thing they believe they need more than they need Jesus.

Surrender to the Lord requires being real. Oswald Chambers says in My Utmost for His Highest says to every degree in which we are not real, we will dispute rather than come to Jesus. When someone runs to anything or anyone but Jesus, their actions indicate they don't trust him. And if they aren't trusting in Him, they are trusting in something else.

New Testament examples of the Pharisees and their relationship to God reveal attitudes and actions that were religious and resistant to God. They thought they had all the answers and missed the only true answer—Jesus. We can learn from them about the fruitlessness of a braced, unreachable heart.

Principles that hold higher value than relationship create form without purpose and tradition without power. The religious spirit is self-imposed control.

Punishing Spirit

The punishing spirit denies the work of the Cross, the Blood of Jesus and the Resurrection as payment for our sin and mistakes. It blocks from receiving amnesty and forgiveness demanding greater payment. Continuing to punish ourselves for the reasons Christ died for us leads to self-destruction. The punishing spirit strikes with a whip entitled "regret," strategically mutilating hope, confidence and encouragement. It rises in contest to the power of Jesus' Blood.

The punishing spirit gateways to *"hope deferred that makes the heart sick"* (Prov.13:12) rather than hope in the finished work of the Cross (Heb. 6:19).

Jesus asks the orphan heart to, *"Come unto me."* The unloving spirit says, *"I can't,"* the religious spirit says, *"I won't,"* the punishing spirit says *"I don't deserve it."*

The antidote for the orphan spirit is experiencing the Holy Spirit. The Holy Spirit also brings the Spirit of Adoption to encircle and fill the orphan heart, calling to surrender to the *"Daddy"* relationship so desperately needed. *"For you did not receive a spirit that makes you a slave again to fear, but you have received the Spirit of sonship. And by him we cry, Abba Father. The Spirit himself testifies with our spirit that we are God's children."* (Romans 8:15,16)

I was sharing with someone about Lazarus (John 11:38-43 being raised from the dead and Jesus instructing the people to remove the old grave clothes. I told them Jesus gives us new life in Him and clothes us in a new identity. She looked down and with tears welled up in her eyes, she said, *"That is frightening to me. If all the old clothes are gone, who will I be?"*

Luke 19 tells of a parable of ten men each given a mina (about 3 months wages) to invest. All but one invests and receives a profit. The one buried the gift out of fear. He placed the gift where he was more comfortable—at the grave. When you are more comfortable at the gravesite than in the Kingdom, you will bury your blessings rather than let them multiply and prosper.

We cannot truly surrender with hands grasping the grave's head stone. We must surrender with hands grasping the Kingdom. Through conflict and pain we can enter the Kingdom and apprehend it. Eph. 5:14 tells us, *"Awake, O sleeper, and rise from the dead, the light shine in your heart to reveal the Kingdom."*

Personally, putting all my trust into Jesus was not nearly as frightening as spending the rest of my life being chased by fear, guilt and shame. My hour of desperation motivated me and I *came to Him*, forgiving and renouncing (coming out of agreement) with all the pledges and vows I made to past emotional, physical, and traumatic relationships. I entered the Dance of Surrender where my heart was vulnerable and God carried me in His arms.

The experience of trusting Him enables me to access His Presence any time. I continue to allow Him to hold me, protect me, and instruct me because now I'm free to let Him love me. David said it so sweetly in Psalm 34:8, *"Taste and see that the Lord is good; blessed is the man who takes refuge in him."*

> **F** – forsaking
> **A** – all
> **I** – I
> **T** – take
> **H** – Him

I once saw a cartoon that adds an illustration. A perplexed and bewildered man stands at the altar for prayer. On one side is an evangelist praying, *"God, help him to let go ... Oh God, help him to let go."* But on the man's other side is different evangelist praying, *"Oh God, help him to hang on ... Oh God, help him to hang on."*

The Dance of Surrender is the loving process whereby we willingly let go of the Old Music and Old Dances while being romanced in the arms of Jesus into Kingdom reality. We let go while we hang on!

Surrender is an opportunity to deal with pain in a different way. How we deal with pain is a lesson in dealing with evil. Rather than looking for an escape it requires actually holding onto the pain long enough to take it to God.

Loss positions you for justice and transparency unleashes breakthrough. The perils and tribulations of living in a fallen world give us an opportunity to press into His Presence.

When we surrender to God, He always gives us something better in exchange. God always trades up! Isaiah 61:3 gives us an example of God's exchange system.

- He gives us a crown of beauty for ashes.
- He gives us the oil of gladness for mourning.
- He gives us a garment of praise for despair.

Yielding

Teach me, Jesus, how to pray
more like you, have your way.
Create the words within my heart,
so from my lips they do impart.
Teach me in the silent hour,
to wait upon your strength and power.
Mold my life like yielding clay
in your footsteps, every day.
Jesus Christ, ever so sweet,
with nail scarred hands and feet,
I bury old self with you this day
and resurrect in power, *your way*.

—*Yvonne Martinez*

Discussing

Experience the Journey Homework Review

Did they finish the homework?

How did they do with it…any trouble understanding the assignment?

What were the difficult parts of the homework?

Who would like to share?

Workbook Chapter 5

Dance of Surrender

*I will both lie down in peace, and sleep, for
you alone, O LORD, make me dwell in safety.*
— Psalm 4:8

Jesus danced the Dance of Surrender so He and His Father would be "One." It was the beginning of Jesus following His Father's direction so in all ways He would be submitted to His Father. The Dance of Surrender is coming out of yourself and into God. It is about trusting Him—allowing Him to lead us into true freedom and peace.

Giving our problems to Jesus requires an emptying of self-will and self-protection. The "coming" must be accompanied with sincere motivation and desire to be rid of our "yuck." Resistance to surrender will drive us to the edge and limit of our own strength.

What does the Old Music and Old Dance offer that generates resistance to surrender? The answers are in the completion of the following statement. Circle the statements that best represent your resistance.

If I keep this trauma-bond relationship in tact I won't have to...

feel, have an identity, face others, be responsible, be authentic, change, tell secrets, be honest, tell my truth, trust, be in reality, be positive, grow, be accountable, have relationships, be mature, risk, have goals, have values, be independent, have freedom, have internal validation, have a purpose, be connected with people or family, have dreams, have hopes, be successful, have faith, live, be in the present, obtain status, make decisions, have needs, have wants, have communication, intimacy with God or...

_____

_____

Surrender can expose and trigger pain of vulnerability as that which we first experienced during the original trauma. Remember, when I was talking about trauma being a forced intrusion into a safe environment? The person in protective mode perceives themselves as now being safe. Protection is a disguise. Any intrusion into that artificially safe place is felt as penetrating and painful.

Define an intrusion into your presumed safe place.

_____
_____
_____

Resistance to intimacy is fortified by our protective barriers. The barriers are fortified by the promises we made to the Old Music and Old Dances.

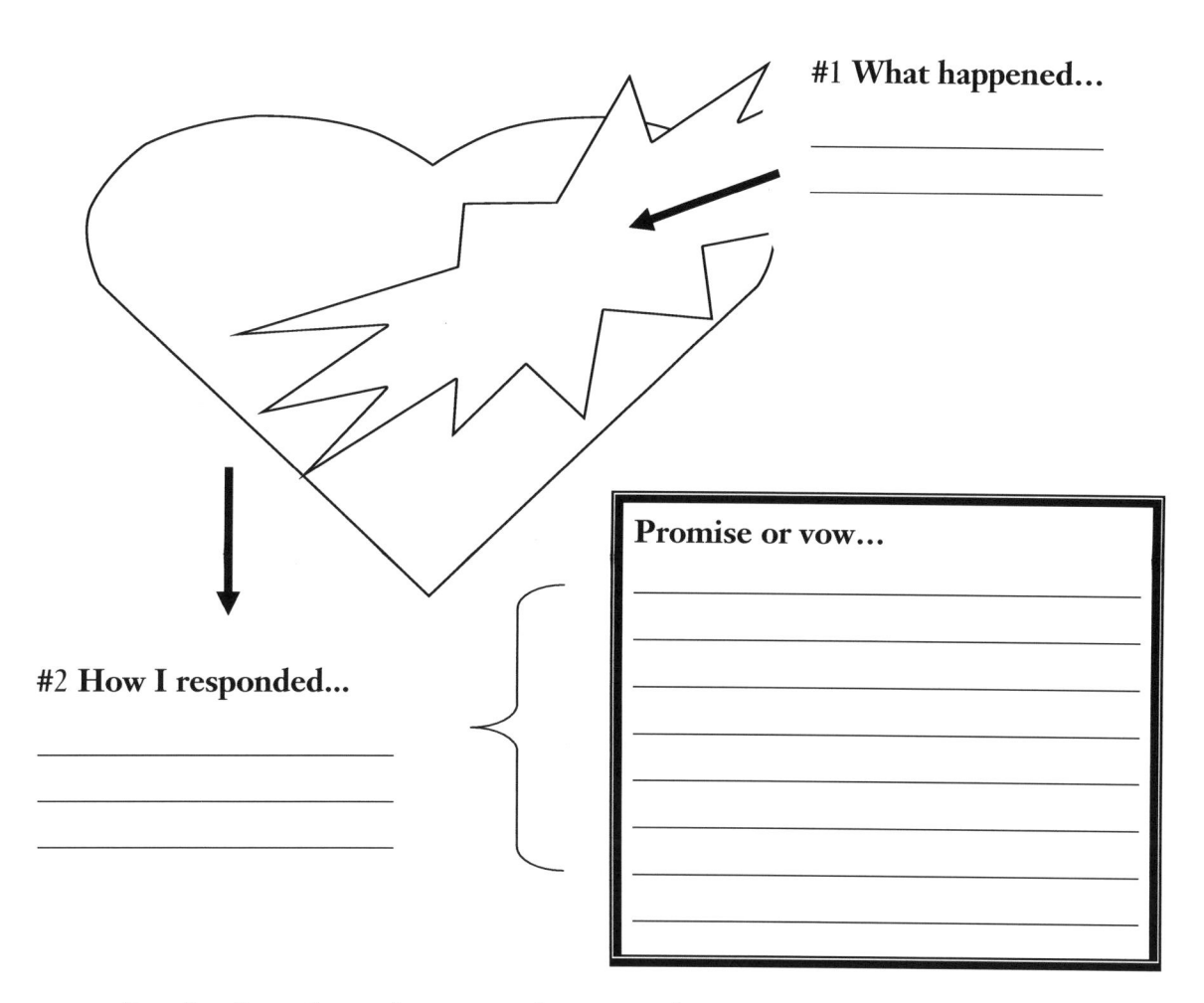

#1 What happened...
_____
_____

#2 How I responded...
_____
_____

Promise or vow...
_____
_____
_____
_____
_____
_____
_____
_____

In the bracket above, write out the promise or vow you made as a result of what happened and your response.

My example..."I made a vow that I didn't need anyone to love me because love hurt.

Read John, Chapter 14

Jesus tells Thomas and the disciples "I will not leave you as orphans...." Jesus discerned Thomas' insecurity and fear.

Jesus identifies an "orphan" spirit manifested in Thomas' fear of being left alone, unprotected, uncovered, rejected and abandoned.

The orphan spirit is drawn through the lack of protection and covering. It only has access because there was an unmet need, a place of trauma and a place of vulnerability. Triggering the pain of vulnerability and the absence of covering, the orphan spirit opens the door to other protectors.

In what way do you identify with an orphan spirit?

Three prominent protectors willingly join the orphan spirit. They are the unloving spirit, the religious spirit and the punishing spirit. If these barriers exist, they must be conquered so surrender will be pure and unhindered, or manipulated.

The Unloving Spirit

The unloving spirit protects the orphaned heart by blocking the ability to give and receive love both from others and God. Its melody plays in harmony with the Old Music, rooted in the past and its footsteps can be tracked throughout the Old Dances. Out of default, the unloving spirit will reject before it gets rejected—it will desire love but behave unlovely.

Love actually brings justice and requires protection. Those who are unable to give and receive love reject the work of the Cross and the Blood of Jesus and thereby reject the "love" God sent them.

The unloving spirit manipulates the orphan heart with unworthiness, pity, condemnation, and justification. It judges, accuses, criticizes and manipulates. It will embrace the comfortably uncomfortable, rather than surrender to God's love.

In what way do you identify with an unloving spirit?

_____
_____
_____
_____
_____
_____
_____
_____
_____
_____
_____
_____
_____
_____
_____
_____
_____
_____
_____
_____

The Religious Spirit

The religious spirit covers the orphaned heart with performance and works. Completing a fifteen-week self-defense course, their lives in neat little packages, and along comes the "invitation" to give it all up! "You must be kidding! I have worked very hard to get where I am and no one is going to take it from me again. Only the strong survive."

The orphaned heart's pain is covered by masks of overeating, oversleeping, overworking, or addictions to pornography, alcohol, drugs, or self-injury. Sometimes the religious spirit is manifested in fear, hiding the orphan heart behind locks, security buildings, police dogs, whistles, or self-defense classes; maybe hiding behind anger, verbal abuse, assault, pride, procrastination and even apathy or hopelessness.

Consequently, the religious spirit is fixated on self-reliance and those things which they can control. Within the Old Music and Old Dance they have created a fortress and any uninvited intrusion reinforces the barriers.

Principles that hold higher value than relationship create form without purpose and tradition without power. The religious spirit is self-imposed control.

In what way do you identify with a religious spirit?

_____
_____
_____
_____
_____
_____
_____
_____

Punishing Spirit

The punishing spirit denies the work of the Cross, the Blood of Jesus and the Resurrection as full and complete payment for our sin and mistakes. It blocks receiving amnesty and forgiveness demanding greater payment. Continuing to punish ourselves for the reasons Christ died for us leads to self-destruction.

The punishing spirit strikes with a whip entitled "regret," strategically mutilating hope, confidence and encouragement. It rises in contest to the power of Jesus' Blood.

The punishing spirit gateways to "hope deferred that makes the heart sick" (Prov.13:12) rather than hope in the finished work of the Cross (Heb. 6:19). It will cause you to feel unworthy of receiving God's healing power.

In what way do you identify with a punishing spirit?

_____
_____
_____
_____
_____
_____
_____
_____
_____
_____
_____
_____
_____

The antidote for the orphan spirit and its allies is experiencing the Holy Spirit. The Holy Spirit, counselor and comforter, brings the Spirit of Adoption to encircle and fill the wounded heart, drawing us into the "Papa, Daddy" relationship so desperately needed.

"For you did not receive a spirit that makes you a slave again to fear, but you have received the Spirit of Sonship. And by him we cry, Abba Father. The Spirit himself testifies with our spirit that we are God's children." (Romans 8:15,16)

Would you like to receive the Spirit of Adoption?

Ask Papa to prepare your heart to receive ...

We cannot truly surrender with hands grasping the grave's head stone. We must surrender with hands grasping the Kingdom. Through conflict and pain we can enter the Kingdom and apprehend it.

> "Awake, O sleeper, and rise from the dead, the light shine in your heart to reveal the Kingdom."
> Eph. 5:14

> "Taste and see that the Lord is good; blessed is the man who takes refuge in him."
> Psalm 34:8,

Surrender is the loving process whereby we willingly let go of the Old Music and Old Dances while being romanced in the arms of Jesus into Kingdom reality. We let go while we hang on!

Surrender is an opportunity to deal with pain in a different way. How we deal with pain is a lesson in dealing with evil. Rather than looking for an escape it requires actually holding onto the pain long enough to take it to God.

Loss positions you for justice and transparency unleashes breakthrough. The perils and tribulations of living in a fallen world give us an opportunity to press into His Presence.

Yielding

Teach me, Jesus, how to pray

more like you, have your way.

Create the words within my heart,

so from my lips they do impart.

Teach me in the silent hour,

to wait upon your strength and power.

Mold my life like yielding clay

in your footsteps, every day.

Jesus Christ, ever so sweet,

with nail scarred hands and feet,

I bury old self with you this day

and resurrect in power, your way.

—Yvonne Martinez

Praying

For the balance of the weeks, center prayer time around those who did not apprehend the teaching or fully understand how to pray through the exercise.

Helps

- **No pressure to surrender, it is an opportunity!**
- **Are there any promises you can't afford to keep?**
- **Anything else to let go of?**
- **Anything else to hang on to?**

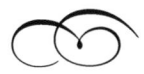

Homework

- Read Chapter 6 in Dancing on the Graves of Your Past book
- Complete Chapter 6 in Dancing on the Graves of Your Past workbook

Handouts

- Practicing Forgiveness Journal Exercise E in Appendix

Do you have any handouts for your group?

10

Week Seven

"Dance of Forgiveness"

"Give, and it will be given to you. A good measure, pressed down, shaken together and running over, will be poured into your lap. For with the measure you use, it will be measured to you."

—Luke 6:38

How to

Call the meeting to order with words of welcome and prayer.

Forgiveness unlocks the prison door. Who wants to open the door and leave the prison cell?

Teaching

Dancing on the Graves of Your Past book

Book Chapter 6

DANCE OF FORGIVENESS

*"Give, and it will be given to you. A good measure,
pressed down, shaken together and running over,
will be poured into your lap. For with the measure you
use, it will be measured to you."*
—Luke 6:38

The Dance of Surrender and The Dance of Forgiveness are necessary for authentic intimacy with Him. They reveal dependency, love and trust, keeping our hearts pure. A life of surrender and forgiveness can follow the lead of the King. These two dances are the antidote for anger, rebellion, offence, and bitterness.

Forgiveness is a fruit of surrender. Those who surrender their lives to God choose to forgive, not because they should, but because they want to. Forgiveness is the courage to let mercy triumph over judgment (James 2:13).

God provided forgiveness for people who were destined to fail but who chose to return to God. In the Old Testament, sin was forgiven through sacrificial offerings. Then God sent his son, Jesus, who for all time *is* the sacrifice for our sins. It is through Jesus we have forgiveness, and because we have been forgiven we can forgive others.

In forgiving, we release our judgment or desire for revenge. Inpatient hospital programs advertise "Forgiveness Therapy" and an employee from a major corporation recently told me it had scheduled "Personal Enrichment" seminars (which included the topic of forgiveness) to increase self-esteem and productivity of employees. These programs are finding out what God has told us all along—there is a connection between forgiveness and good mental health.

Forgiveness was God's idea so it is no surprise we have many Biblical examples and instructions about God's forgiveness or our forgiving others.

In fact, *Strong's Exhaustive Concordance of the Bible (NIV version)* lists 102 verses that use the words *forgive, forgiven,* or *forgiveness! (NIV version)*

In Matthew 18:21-35, Jesus tells us a parable about a master who cancels a great debt owed by his servant. The servant, in turn, refuses to extend mercy to his debtor. When the master learns about this, he becomes angry and turns the servant over to be tortured until he pays back all he owed. Then Jesus says, *"This is how my heavenly Father will treat each of you unless you forgive your brother from your heart."*

We have been released from a great eternal judgment for our sins, given a new birth, the Kingdom and eternal life. God wants us to forgive because He has forgiven us. He wants us to show mercy because He has shown us mercy. Extending mercy is no longer desiring that others will get what they deserve.

Giving forgiveness to those who hurt us

When we experience the grace of God's forgiveness we forgive others more freely. We choose to release from our judgment those who have hurt us, and we choose to show mercy toward them. Releasing others from our prideful judgment releases us from the pain and emotional torture unforgiveness produces. When we forgive, God releases us and we release ourselves.

Think of a fish caught on a hook. As the fish struggles and struggles, the hook penetrates deeper into the fish. As long as the fish focuses on the fisherman and the struggle, the hook twists and turns in its flesh. The struggle causes more pain for the fish than for the fisherman. When the fish forgives, it cuts the line and stops the struggle with the fisherman. Forgiveness sets the fish free. Afterward, the fish can get the hook out allowing the wound to heal.

Giving forgiveness to those who are not sorry

Often we want to set up conditions or see remorse on someone's part before we will forgive them. Sometimes we want them to "suffer the consequences" of their behavior so we withhold forgiveness. This really means our forgiveness is conditioned upon the guilty party's repentance. We say, "*If you're sorry, I'll forgive you.*" Jesus says, "*I forgive you,*" which causes us to feel sorry. Jesus' forgiveness and mercy invites our repentance. When we forgive, we let go of our connection to their behavior. This actually allows the other person freedom to wrestle with their heart issues.

Giving forgiveness when you don't feel like it

When hurt hasn't been addressed, forgiveness will seem detached from feelings.

It is like looking into a closet that has been cluttered for a long time. Every time you open the closet door you see the mess and feel bad. You will never enjoy the good feelings that come from having a clean closet while you are still looking at the mess. Just as soon as you begin working on the mess and the closet is finally clean, the good feelings of relief and release come naturally.

When you obey God and clean out the clutter of unforgiveness, you are drawn closer into the next dance —the Dance of the Overcomer.

Giving forgiveness to those who persist in abusing you

Whoever hurts you or abuses you, a Christian, is guilty of sin against God's temple (1Cor. 3:16; 6:19). Allowing them to continue hurting you is not good for them and, of course, not good for you. In every case that Jesus endured or submitted to persecution, it was to bring glory to his Father. Likewise, our submission should bring glory to God or cause others to be drawn to Christ.

When David (1 Samuel) was persecuted and pursued by Saul, he removed himself from the violence. On two occasions, David spared Saul's life when he could have killed him in defense. If David had retaliated, he would have been no better than Saul. David was able to leave Saul in God's hands, and God honored David.

Relationships that continue to damage you emotionally or physically need to be handled with the same maturity. You can remove yourself from the abuse and the abuser. Forgiveness doesn't mean you can or should continue in relationship with people who aren't safe or who aren't trustworthy.

Giving forgiveness when you are angry

Being angry is not a sin, but extended hostility, insult, or injury is. Anger has active expressions like yelling, throwing things or hitting people. It also has passive expressions like forget-fullness, procrastination, or apathy. You know anger is a sin when you see its negative responses and reflection in the faces of others we have hurt.

Asking forgiveness for our offenses

When we confess our sins (and unforgiveness is a sin), God will forgive us. This forgiveness is guaranteed through Jesus. When possible, we also need to ask for forgiveness from those we have directly or indirectly hurt.

Asking for forgiveness when someone refuses to forgive

Your asking for forgiveness is an act of obedience and shows responsibility as well as maturity, but you cannot dictate what the response might be. The act of asking for forgiveness releases the one you've wounded. Your asking for forgiveness cuts the line from you, the fisher, to the fish. Your asking for forgiveness gives up your struggle with the fish by you cutting the line and the fish is set free. How they handle their freedom is not your responsibility.

Receiving forgiveness for our offenses

If we don't forgive ourselves, we haven't truly believed God has forgiven us and we continue to punish ourselves for the things Christ died for. This action tells God that Jesus sacrifice is insufficient payment for our mistakes or sins.

We may have failed but we are not a failure. We cannot do anything to remedy our shame and guilt. Jesus alone can remove them through His atonement. There is a cleansing (1 John 1:9) and healing (Ps. 103:3 and Ps. 147:3) element associated with God's forgiveness. The purity of Jesus' shed Blood washes us, not just covering over, but removing any stain or odor, any residue or evidence. Receiving forgiveness is partnering with God's love.

Unforgiveness

Unforgiveness keeps the door open to the pain of trauma. It also leaves the door open to anger, hatred, bitterness, rebellion, and murder. Unforgiveness is holding an ungodly power against or over someone.

The premise is if resolution or a reduction in intensity of the memory was to take place, then emotional connection would diminish and stop the ability to have control or cease the ability to seek revenge against those who hurt them.

I visited a Christian woman while hospitalized for a nervous breakdown. Five years earlier she had been raped by a man she knew and trusted. When I asked her about forgiveness, she said she would *never* forgive him for what he did. Unforgiveness held open the door to the trauma so she could revisit anytime and find ways for revenge. The open door also allowed him to mentally rape her over and over.

This conversation came to my mind one evening when I was making dinner. Opening a can of tomatoes and pouring them into a pan, I could smell the tomatoes had a bad odor. Looking into the empty container I saw corrosion on the inside of the can. I checked the outside of the can and found it had been dented. I realized the dent caused the contents to spoil.

The Lord showed me that this is how unforgiveness is in our hearts. Our unforgiveness is like acid in a fragile cup. A blow to the outside damages the delicate contents and corrodes the inside of the container.

The forgiver pays a great price and the guilty goes free. This is the example that Christ gave us. He forgave and we go free. There is no other payment for our guilt.

Unforgiveness will never remedy a wrong or fix the problem. Wrong doing, even when forgiven, may have perpetuated consequences that we no longer have the power to control or change. In most cases the emotional or physical damage is either irreparable or irreplaceable. Likewise, we forgive because repayment is impossible and unforgiveness is a death-grip on pain.

What Forgiveness Isn't

Forgiveness is essential to healing, releasing us from the pain of torment. But forgiveness isn't denying the pain, excusing the crime or guaranteeing reconciliation.

Forgiveness isn't denying the pain

Sally was taken into the woods and tortured by a boyfriend. He cut off her arms and wrapped her with duct tape. Sally managed to get to the road and was rescued by a driver. Forgiveness doesn't erase Sally's need for medical attention. Although this is a profound example, it makes the point. The brutal physical wounds from Sally's attack aren't healed when she forgives her attacker. There remains the process of learning how to live her life in the aftermath of this tragedy. Forgiveness is essential, but we may be faced with physical and emotional pain that needs further healing to put lives back on track.

In the fishing scenario, after the line was cut, the hook in the fish still needed to be removed so the wound could heal.

Forgiveness isn't excusing the crime

Jesus acknowledged the repentant thief hanging on the cross next to Him. In Jesus' compassion toward the thief, Jesus told the thief he would be in paradise that day with Jesus (Luke 42:43). However, the thief still died for his crime.

My husband, Tony, led a prison ministry. Every service he ministered to men who were forgiven by Christ, yet who were still serving their sentences. Forgiveness rectifies the spiritual judgment, but it doesn't necessarily absolve from the restitution required according to our moral, judicial or governmental laws.

Forgiveness isn't reconciliation

Forgiving doesn't mean you will, or can, have relationship with the ones you forgive. My father died before I became a Christian. Forgiveness couldn't reconcile our relationship, but I have the peace of knowing I let go of my hurt and anger. Through Christ, I was able to forgive him for his rejection and abandonment.

In the example of David and Saul, it wasn't safe for David to remain close to Saul (1 Sam. 19:1). David was willing, but Saul's attitude and actions stood in the way of their relationship. If Saul had been willing to change, the story would have had a much different ending.

Forgiveness isn't reconciliation, but it's a beginning

Today's language would describe David as detaching himself from Saul and establishing healthy boundaries. For David, relationship with Saul was never re-established. David remained pure in heart and in 2 Samuel, Chapter 1, David was sincerely grieved at Saul's death and honored Saul for the greatness of Saul's life.

The goal for David, and for us, is to back up, catch our breath, redesign our plan, and merge back into our lives as ambassadors of Christ Jesus.

Returning to the fishing metaphor, we need to cut the line, remove the hook, and doctor our wounds. During this process we learn valuable lessons about where the fisher fishes and what bait he uses. Learning healthy boundaries helps to ensure we activate the tools needed for building safe relationships.

Reconciliation with the fisherman may not be possible or safe but we will swim along happier because forgiveness *will* guarantee reconciliation with God.

Anger

Anger, like unforgiveness keeps open connection to the trauma, allowing entry back into the event, reinforcing the bonding. Anger is a futile attempt to control a situation that has been out of control.

Rachel emptied the trash after a party and forgot to lock the back door. Later the evening a man entered the house, sexually assaulted and attempted to rape her. I first met with Rachel about three months after the attack. Rachel finished the story. During the sexual assault Rachel began to tell the man he didn't have to hurt her because Jesus loved him. The man stopped and ran from the house. With Rachel's help, her identification and willingness to come forward in trial, the assailant was caught and convicted. Rachel felt peace with the way she handled the situation.

Rachel's problem was with her fiancé. He repeatedly questioned Rachel about why she didn't lock the door and continually wanted her to restate exactly what the attacker did to her sexually. He was unable to resolve anger over his fiancé having been sexually violated. Injustice attracts anger, but anger isn't a remedy for injustice.

We also need to resolve the question of anger towards God. It's often easier to forgive a person than to forgive God. After all, God is well aware of the events that happened in our life, and yet, circumstances didn't change. If we become embittered with God we will build a shell of resistance that will insulate us from His presence.

Often I receive calls from someone wrestling with the questions: *"Where was God when this happened and why didn't he stop it?"* I had to personally settle these same questions for myself and so will you.

God is good. God is love. A good, loving God does not order disaster into our life to teach us a lesson. He wasn't out to lunch when bad things happened. God doesn't send us diseases to make us better Christians. The source of affliction is our enemy who uses bad circumstances to build a case of unbelief against God. However, God will use the circumstances to draw us to Him, if we will come.

Jesus suffered and paid the price for our healing and freedom. Jesus was the remedy for God's wrath and the substitute for God's punishment. Jesus took our suffering upon Himself. Jesus died so we could live emotionally, physically, spiritually, and eternally free with full access to the benefits of a good, loving God. If we believe anything less we will create a theology that resists or opposes the truth. Because of Jesus, we are unpunishable.

I couldn't fix myself and neither could any other person. My pain, although not caused by God, created my awareness of need for Him. In retrospect, I can see and experience good that came from the bad. My experiences taught me that I must trust in Him no matter what the circumstances look like.

We live and contend with unanswered mystery. The uncomfortableness of contending with mystery creates doctrines and theologies to soothe our minds.

Whatever grace we receive to access doors of revelation is received in relationship with Him. The truth that sets you free will never be found through mental gymnastics or religious principles. So, don't be led through a maze, a journey inward, to find the answers to your problems.

Our minds don't contain the answers, Jesus does. The answer must be found outside of ourselves, in a journey to discover Him.

Discussing

Experience the Journey Homework Review

Did they finish the homework?

How did they do with it…any trouble understanding the assignment?

Who would like to share?

Workbook Chapter 6

Dance of Forgiveness

"Give, and it will be given to you. A good measure,
pressed down, shaken together and running over,
will be poured into your lap. For with the measure you
use, it will be measured to you."
—Luke 6:38

Surrender and forgiveness are necessary for authentic intimacy with Him. They reveal dependency, love and trust, keeping our hearts pure. Forgiveness is a fruit of surrender. In forgiving, we release our judgment or desire for revenge. Forgiveness is the courage to let mercy triumph over judgment.

Read James 2:13

What is your response to the paragraphs in *Dancing on the Graves of Your Past*, pages 143 – 149?

Giving forgiveness to those who hurt us

_____
_____
_____
_____
_____

Giving forgiveness to those who are not sorry

_____
_____
_____
_____
_____

Giving forgiveness when you don't feel like it

_____
_____
_____
_____
_____

Giving forgiveness to those who persist in abusing you

_____
_____
_____
_____
_____

Giving forgiveness when you are angry

_____
_____
_____
_____
_____

What is your response to the paragraphs in *Dancing on the Graves of Your Past*, pages 157 - 162?

Forgiveness isn't denying the pain

_____
_____
_____

Forgiveness isn't excusing the crime

_____
_____
_____

Forgiveness isn't reconciliation

_____
_____
_____

Forgiveness isn't reconciliation, but it is a start

_____
_____
_____

Read 1John 1:9, Psalm 103:3, and 147:3

What is God showing you about these scriptures?

_____
_____
_____
_____
_____

There is a cleansing and healing element associated with God's forgiveness. The purity of Jesus' shed Blood washes us, not just covering over, but removing any stain or odor, any residue or evidence. Receiving forgiveness is partnering with God's love.

Prayer

"Papa God, I want to partner with Your love. I no longer want to hold unforgiveness in my heart. I am ready to surrender and let go of anything holding me back from receiving all You have for me."

"Papa God, who do I need to forgive?" Write down the first names of the people He shows you.

_____
_____
_____
_____
_____

For each person He reveals, use the following prayer format…

"I forgive _____ *for*

(listen to what the Lord shows you before you fill in the blanks)

_____
_____
_____

I confess I have carried judgment and offence. I ask forgiveness for my actions of _____*."*

I hand this person to You…

Do a prophetic act and actually hand off and release them to God.

After you finish forgiving those He shows you, ask...

"Papa God, now that I have forgiven, what do You have for me in exchange?"

What did He give you?

_____
_____
_____
_____
_____
_____
_____

How do you feel now?

_____
_____
_____
_____
_____
_____
_____
_____

What do good boundaries look like for those relationships that are still difficult or unsafe?

*"Have mercy on me, O God, according to your unfailing love;
according to your great compassion blot out my transgressions.
Wash away all my iniquity and cleanse me from my sin."*
Ps. 51:1, 2

For each of your own protective actions or behavior attitudes, ask Papa to forgive you for any way you trusted in the protector and didn't trust Him.

"Papa God, You have known my heart all along and never stopped loving me, even when I wasn't able to trust You. Thank You for showing me how the protective behavior/attitude of

_____

*has kept me from being closer to You.
Please forgive me for*

_____,

setting me free from guilt and shame, according to Your Word.

I come out of agreement with the need for this protector/behavior and renounce the ungodly or unholy alliance. I hand

_____

to You and tell it bye-bye…so long!"

Is there anything you would like to add to your prayer?

_____
_____
_____

Now ask Him, *"Papa God, do You forgive me?"*

What did He say?

_____
_____
_____

Do you accept Papa God's forgiveness?

_____
_____
_____

If so, then write it out... *"Yes, Papa God, I accept Your forgiveness, mercy, and love."*

_____
_____

Now ask, *"Papa God, what do You have for me in exchange?"*

_____
_____
_____
_____

Is there anything you want to add to your prayer?

_____
_____
_____

Write anything additional Papa is showing you...

_____
_____
_____
_____
_____

For any way you have hurt others because of your protective actions or behavior attitudes, ask Papa to forgive you.

"Papa God, You have known my heart all along and never stopped loving me, even when I took out my pain on others. Thank You for showing me how the protective behavior/attitude of

_____

has hurt others and created barriers in personal relationships. Please forgive me for

_____,

setting me free from guilt and shame, according to Your Word.

I come out of agreement with the need to blame or shame others through this protector/behavior and renounce the ungodly or unholy alliance.

I hand

_____

to You and tell it bye-bye...so long!"

Is there anything you would like to add to your prayer?

_____
_____
_____

Now ask Him, *"Papa God, do You forgive me?"*
What did He say?

_____
_____
_____

Do you accept Papa God's forgiveness?

_____
_____

If so, then write it out... "*Yes, Papa God, I accept Your forgiveness, mercy, and love.*"

_____
_____

Now ask, *"Papa God, what do You have for me in exchange?"*

_____
_____
_____
_____

Is there anything you want to add to your prayer?

_____
_____
_____

Write anything additional Papa is showing you...

_____
_____
_____
_____

Secrets and False Power...

"Papa, I ask You to forgive me for carrying secrets or for believing I have the power to cause people to behave in a certain way, both are types of false power. I come out of agreement with the belief that I have supernatural power outside of You.

I renounce saying anything "was my fault" if it wasn't my fault and come out of agreement with any form of witchcraft that would have led me to believe I have power over anyone."

What is Papa showing you now?

_____
_____
_____
_____

Forgiving yourself is sometimes the most difficult. Ask Papa God... *"Am I holding anything against myself?"* **Write what He shows you.**

"Papa, God, what do I need to forgive myself for?"

Ask Papa God to give you a picture of yourself at the time of the event (you identified this age when you first recorded the event). You will use this picture as a focal point for prayer. After God gives you a picture of yourself, hold onto that image and answer the following...

How old are you in the picture? _____

How were you feeling?

_____
_____
_____
_____
_____
_____
_____
_____
_____

Using the image as a point of prayer…

" *(your name)* _____, *I forgive you for*

(write as many things as Papa shows you)

My example: Yvonne, I forgive you for being needy, for feeling lonely, for misbehaving for attention…

_____
_____
_____
_____
_____

_____

And

I ask you to forgive me for judging you, being angry with you, rejecting you, shaming you, disconnecting from you, even hating you…
(finish in your own words)

_____
_____
_____
_____
_____
_____
_____

When you feel ready, continue with the following

"(your name) _____, I a sorry for the things I have held against you and I am sorry for not allowing you to be cleansed and washed by Jesus Blood…I now invite you now to receive Jesus Blood to wash and cover you…(pause for His presence to meet with you) and I invite you back into my heart."

After you have finished forgiving yourself, ask Papa God what He wants to give you in exchange…write down what He gives you!

_____
_____

How do you feel now?

The truth is that Jesus died for every issue in your life. You are just now receiving His Blood, His Love, His Forgiveness, and His Mercy into those areas you previously felt were unworthy of His redemption.

Wait to listen for anything additional God wants to tell you and write it down.

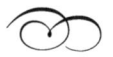

Breaking Soul Ties

- If there has been a dysfunctional ungodly or unholy relationship with this person such as co-dependency, people pleasing, poor boundaries, continued thinking about them or the situation, idolatry, etc...

- If there was sexual relationship, whether it was abuse or consensual, forgiving the person and breaking soul ties is important...

When you break soul ties you are cutting off, in the spirit, an ungodly and unholy alliance to a person or situation. Whether you were aware of this or not, these connections can establish priority and your allegiance to them creates an obstacle to freedom.

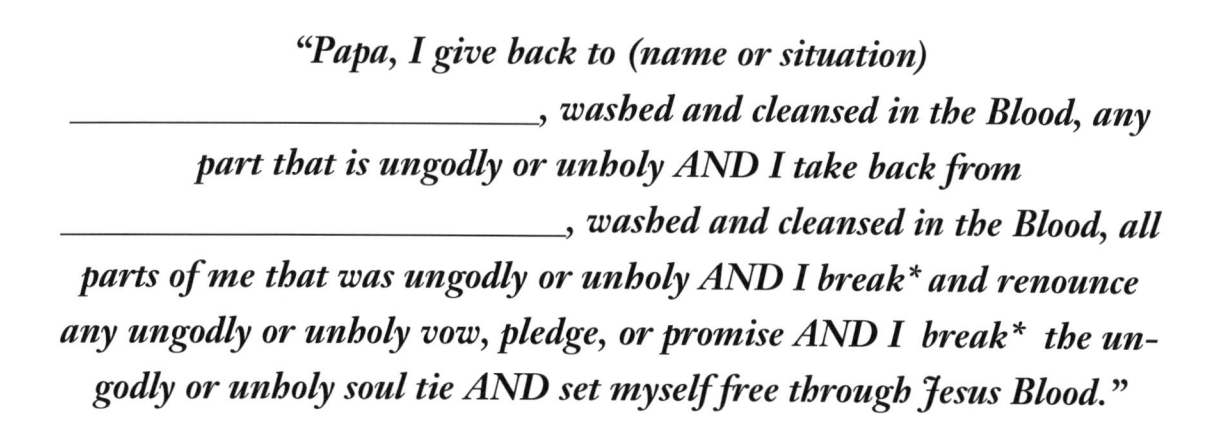

"Papa, I give back to (name or situation) _____, washed and cleansed in the Blood, any part that is ungodly or unholy AND I take back from _____, washed and cleansed in the Blood, all parts of me that was ungodly or unholy AND I break* and renounce any ungodly or unholy vow, pledge, or promise AND I break* the ungodly or unholy soul tie AND set myself free through Jesus Blood."

***NOTE: When you say the word "break", in any of the prayers, I want you to do a prophetic act and clap as loud as you can...this declaration shifts the atmosphere and makes an announcement on your behalf!*

- If there are generational sins or curses…

"Papa, I stand in repentance on behalf of past generations for the sins of

_____

and ask for forgiveness on their behalf.

I come out of agreement on behalf of past generations and come out of agreement for the sins

of

_____.

AND break* the word curses

of

_____

off myself, my generation and the generations to come..
I give back to those generations (name or situation) _____, washed and cleansed in the Blood, any part that was ungodly or unholy AND I take back from those generations (name or situation) _____, washed and cleansed in the Blood, all vows, pledges, promises that were ungodly or unholy AND I break* and renounce any word curse AND I break* the ungodly or unholy soul tie AND set myself and my family free, my generation and the generations to come, through Jesus Blood."

We also need to resolve the question of anger towards God. It's often easier to forgive a person than to forgive God. After all, God is well aware of the events that happened in our life, and yet, circumstances didn't change. If we become embittered with God we will build a shell of resistance that will insulate us from His presence.

God is good. God is love. A good, loving God does not order disaster into our life to teach us a lesson. He wasn't out to lunch when bad things happened.

God doesn't send us diseases to make us better Christians. The source of affliction is our enemy who uses bad circumstances to build a case of unbelief against God. However, God will use the circumstances to draw us to Him, if we will come.

Jesus suffered and paid the price for our healing and freedom. Jesus was the remedy for God's wrath and the substitute for God's punishment. Jesus took our suffering upon Himself. Jesus died so we could live emotionally, physically, spiritually, and eternally free with full access to the benefits of a good, loving God.

Ask Papa God to forgive you for blaming Him.

_____
_____
_____
_____
_____
_____
_____

"Papa God, what is the truth?"

_____
_____
_____
_____
_____
_____
_____
_____
_____
_____
_____
_____
_____
_____
_____

The truth that sets you free will never be found through mental gymnastics or religious principles. So, don't be led through a maze, a journey inward, to find the answers to your problems.

Our minds don't contain the answers, Jesus does. The answer must be found outside of ourselves, in a journey to discover Him.

Praying

For the balance of the weeks, center prayer time around those who did not apprehend the teaching or fully understand how to pray through the exercise.

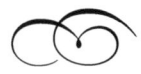

Helps

I told God I was angry.

I thought He'd be surprised.

I thought I'd kept hostility

Quite cleverly disgised.

I told the Lord I hate Him

I told Him that I was hurt.

I told Him that He isn't fair.

He's treated me like dirt.

I told God I was angry

But I'm the one surprised.

"What I've known all along," He said,

"You've finally realized."

"At last you have admitted

What's really in your heart.

Dishonesty, not anger,

Was keeping us apart."

"Even when you hate Me,

I don't stop loving you.

Before you can receive that love

You must confess what's true."

"In telling Me the anger

You genuinely feel,

It loses power over you,

Permitting you to heal."

I told God I was sorry

And He's forgiven me

The truth that I was angry

Has finally set me free.

Permission to print given by writer, Jessica Shaver)

Homework

- Read Chapter 7 in Dancing on the Graves of Your Past book
- Complete Chapter 7 in Dancing on the Graves of Your Past workbook

Handouts

What other information does your group need to supplement the teaching or discussion? Anything you want to give them as they prepare for next week?

- Handling Your Thoughts Journal Exercise F in Appendix.

11

Week Eight
"Dance of the Overcomer"

*The Lord is faithful, and he will strengthen and
protect you from the evil one.*
—2 Thessalonians 3:3

How to

Call the meeting to order with prayer. The subject of spiritual warfare is varied. Keep focused on teaching. We are not looking for a demon under every rock. We also don't want to ignore the enemy or the battle. The purpose of war is to win victoriously!

Teaching

Dancing on the Graves of Your Past book

Book Chapter 7

Dance of the Overcomer

The Lord is faithful, and he will strengthen and protect you from the evil one.
—2 Thessalonians 3:3

We are His chosen, His friend, the object of His affection and attention. The Dance of the Overcomer is taking possession of your position in Him. This is not only freedom from your past but freedom to engage your destiny.

In Song of Songs 2:9,10 the "lover" comes to the "beautiful one" to arouse her from a place of comfort. The lover invites the beautiful one out from behind her wall to join Him as He, like a gazelle, bounds from mountain top to mountain top, conquering the "high places" signifying His dominion over things that have exalted themselves against the knowledge of God. We join Him as a partner in the Dance of the Overcomer, no longer walking on His feet, but our hand in His hand and close by His side.

For the beloved to accept the invitation to this dance, she must come out from behind her wall.

"But we all, with unveiled face, beholding as in a mirror the glory of the Lord, are being transformed into the same image from glory to glory, just as by the Spirit of the Lord." (2 Cor. 3:19) The veil (any protective covering) needs to be removed so we can go from "glory to glory."

He doesn't break down the wall or rip off the veil. He doesn't kidnap her against her will. Rather, it is a partnership whereby she willingly joins him. Accepting the invitation, He takes her on a journey appearing much like Superman and Jane! He begins to teach her about conquering and overcoming, dominion and authority. These next verses from 2 Corinthians tell me if we are in a war and we have weapons, we must have an enemy!

"For though we live in the world, we do not wage war as the world does. The weapons we fight with are not the weapons of the world. On the contrary, they have divine power to demolish strongholds. We demolish arguments and every pretension that sets itself up against the knowledge of God, and we take captive every thought to make it obedient to Christ." (2 Cor. 10:3-5)

The warfare is a spiritual war that began when Satan first rebelled against God and God exiled him from heaven. We are told (John 14:30) that Satan now sits as the prince of this world. An important fact here is that Satan is only a prince and is subject to the King! When Jesus took the keys to hell and death, Satan's reign as prince was trumped by the King's reign!

Jesus destroyed the works of the devil so you would have full access to immunity and authority—life more abundant as described in John 10:10. I love Kris Valloton's statement, *"The purpose of war is victory, the purpose of victory is occupation and the purpose of occupation is inhabitation."* Jesus won the war to give you victory so you could occupy and inhabit the Kingdom *"on earth as it is in heaven"* (Matt. 6:10).

The territory of dominion given to Adam and Eve must have had spiritual boundaries. They were given authority to expand and subdue the earth. This means the land outside the paradise of Eden was not subdued. Adam and Eve were given the authority to overpower, conquer, discipline, tame, and restrain to expand and enlarge the territory of Eden.

Similarly, the promised land of Canaan, the land the Israelites were to inhabit, was left in the hands of giants (Numbers 13:28). The Israelites had to enter and overpower, conquer, discipline, tame and restrain the land before they could occupy, expand, and enjoy its bounty and fruit.

In both these examples, God had given the people the land, commission to move forward, and the authority to occupy. However, in both situations the enemies who previously occupied the land needed to be conquered.

When Jesus resurrected from the grave, He took the keys to hell and death (Rev. 1:18) and gave them to us (Matt. 16:19). The keys were to unlock access to the Kingdom of God so it would be *"on earth as it is in heaven."* In essence, the reinstatement of Jesus' authority to destroy the works of the devil (1John 3:8) has now been passed on to us. We have been given His authority to expand the Kingdom of God on earth and legally take back territory that has been occupied by the enemy.

Land filled with giants or land filled with milk and honey? After exploring Canaan, the men came back with different reports. Caleb was focused on taking possession of the land with confidence saying, "*...for we can do it.*" (Num. 13:30) In contrast, other men shrunk back in fear with a bad report saying the people of the land were of great size and devour those living in it.

Spiritual warfare is taking back the territory and coming into agreement with the good report, *we can do it!* We take back the land given to us—for us *and* our future generations. What feels like an attack is actually enemy resistance because you entered the territory where he has his couch and refrigerator! It is the place he has made his home. We initiate the conflict to assert the dominion and authority of God.

Since it is a spiritual war, natural or "carnal" weapons are ineffective. The shields and swords of the Old Music and Old Dances don't work on a spiritual enemy.

Denying acknowledgment of an enemy is equally unwise as blaming him for everything. However, the warfare is real and persistent. We have a genuine enemy who will push us to fail, shrink back, and fall.

Discipline and self-control aren't enough to change spiritual atmospheres. A good example is the person addicted to alcohol or food. They can stop excess consumption through will power, but the heart will still be hurting and the enemy will still occupy a stronghold. No one can "white knuckle" their way to inner freedom.

Freedom isn't something we *do*; it must be who we *are*. This hits precisely at the core of our enemies attack —the opposition against our identity in Him. It was the source of doubt used against Eve, it was the source of temptation against Jesus in the wilderness, and it was the source of fear that pricked Thomas' orphan heart.

Satan forfeited his relationship with God. He is no longer part of the Kingdom of God. He is no longer in the inner circle of the Angels that surround the Throne. He is no longer in worship and adoration of God. He is separated from God. He wants us to be like him.

Great military strategist plan their offence and defense before firing their weapons. We also learn what fortifies enemy strongholds. In the enemy's game there is no love, no mercy, and no forgiveness. He is a liar and the father of lies (John 8:44).

A liar, like a lion, stalks his prey

Satan cannot be everywhere and doesn't know everything. However, he's been around long time and sees us and our world from a different vantage point. He unfairly uses unguarded moments of trauma, fear, hatred, occult or sexual sin. He watches and waits for vulnerability and wounding and the places we have believed lies. He is an opportunist, using the lies against us to strengthen his stronghold.

A liar disguises

He often appears with an approachable demeanor. He came to Eve in the form of a serpent (Gen. 3:1) and as an angel of light (2 Cor. 11:14). When we aren't looking to God to meet our needs, the enemy can become what we think we need.

A liar destroys

He attacks through the circumstances, placing a wedge between Christians and their faith. Satan's goal is to destroy a Christians' relationship with God, their effectiveness and influence.

A liar defends

His claim is stacked with doubt, deception, and delusion. His progressive success creates a stronghold, an area of predominance.

A liar plants doubt

Satan's first move against Eve was to plant skepticism or disbelief in her mind about the character of God.

A liar plants deception

Satan uses deliberate concealment or misrepresentation by adding just enough mixture of truth to make it palatable. He told Eve, she would *"be like God, knowing good and evil"* (Gen. 3:4). She *was* already like God in that she was made in His image AND she *would* very quickly know good and evil. These were truths he twisted to manipulate.

A liar plants delusion

Satan wants to deposit his rebellion and self-will. Eve's belief (agreement) she needed what satan's lie offered rendered her unable to detect falsehood or make sound judgment.

A liar fears truth

His loss comes when his tactics and defense, built on lies, is shattered by the Spirit of Truth. Satan's stronghold is camped in the mind of those who don't know who they are in Christ Jesus. That is why we are to *"be transformed by the renewing of our minds."* (Ro. 12:22)

Underneath the lie is a wound, a hurtful place, and when the demonic has encapsulated both the wound and the lie, it shields the lie from the truth. I know ministries that make the mistake of trying to tackle wounds, lies, and demons with the same approach. Healing of wounds, exposure of lies, and abolishment of demons are different issues and need to be approached from different strategies.

If you make a fist with one hand and then tightly place your other hand over the fist, you have a visual of what I mean. The fist is the wound. The other hand is the enemy encircling the wound. The magnet holding the enemy attached to the wound is the lie. If deliverance methods are used on wounds, more trauma or spiritual abuse is possible. Additionally, it is ineffective to counsel a demon! You don't heal a demon and you don't deliver a wound. Wounds need healing and demons are eliminated through deliverance.

At the core between a wound and the demonic is a lie, like mayonnaise between two slices of bread! In 2 Cor. 10:5 we are told to demolish arguments and every pretension that sets itself up against the knowledge of God and to take captive every thought to make it obedient to Christ. While the demonic is in direct opposition to God, it uses the lie to exalt itself against God. When the lie gets dissolved, the wound can be separated from the demonic and dealt with accordingly. John 8:32 reminds us that when we know the truth, the truth will set us free.

The Dance of the Overcomer is coming out of agreement with the lies and into partnership with Jesus as a "son" and an "heir."

Handling Our Thoughts

Being confronted by our thoughts and feelings isn't necessarily negative. The source can be promptings from the Holy Spirit leading us into truth or our mind rehearsing conversations or events (self-talk), or the enemy's attempt to throw us off course. Thoughts that linger and persist consume our productivity, demanding our attention. They are usually thoughts that strike a vulnerable or unresolved emotional area and become a trigger point.

When the thought is persistent, you don't know the source or can't resolve it, challenge it with the following process.

Is this condemnation or conviction?

Condemnation is from the enemy. It produces false guilt with spiritual death as a goal. It overshadows and points to mistakes or sin. Condemnation's motive is an invitation to resurrect the gravesite of your past, returning to relationship with the Old Music and Old Dances.

Conviction is from the Holy Spirit. It produces true guilt with holiness as a goal. It overshadows and points to mistakes or sin. Conviction's motive invites you to surrender the situation to the gravesite and return your focus on the resurrected Christ in you uniting in relationship with Him.

Is this temptation or a test?

Temptation is from the enemy. Its goal is sin and separation from God. The attractive package contains handcuffs. If you indulge, the attraction will turn to distraction and condemnation will scream accusations.

A test is from God. Its goal is Christian character and draws us closer to God. Tests are often lessons in stewardship. They don't always feel good but ultimately work for our good.

Resolution

If the thoughts are from Old Music or Old Dances and have been surrendered, you've asked for forgiveness and you have forgiven others, then stand firm, rejecting the lie.

If you are not sure, pray about it immediately. Resolve the guilt by accepting any of your personal responsibility. Ask and receive God's forgiveness.

If it is something you are not responsible for, then place responsibility where it belongs then surrender and forgive. Resist and stand firm, rejecting the lie.

You can keep a journal with dates as a memorial to your journey in healing. Discerning the voice of the Good Shepherd is important. Jesus tells us that we will know His voice (John 10:14). Discernment protects you from receiving a false comforter or self-protective behavior which is a lie baited with pain, stress or fear, etc.

The voice of the Good Shepherd will always *lead* you. The voice of another will *drive* you. Refuse to follow the voice of "another." Allow the Spirit of Truth, who is in you, to keep your motives pure. Being tempted does not mean you are sinning. Remember, Jesus was tempted and refuted the lies with truth.

Learn your trigger points. What are the circumstances that cause you to lose your peace? If you feel triggered, a key is to ask God to show you what He wants you to know about yourself and that situation. Then surrender, forgive and renounce any lies, receive His truth.

Revelation opens the door to access. I love the promise at the close of Matthew 14:35-36, *"And when the men of that place recognized Jesus, they sent word to all the surrounding country. People brought all their sick to him and begged him to let the sick just touch the edge of his cloak, and all who touched him were healed."* When we recognize Jesus, we touch him, and we are healed.

Discussing

Experience the Journey Homework Review

Did they finish the homework?

How did they do with it…any trouble understanding the assignment?

After writing their story,

> Were there any patterns they recognized?

> What did they learn new?

Who would like to share?

Workbook Chapter 7

Dance of the Overcomer

*The Lord is faithful, and he will strengthen and
protect you from the evil one.*
—2 Thessalonians 3:3

In Song of Songs 2:9,10 the "lover" comes to the "beautiful one" to arouse her from a place of comfort.

What do these verses say to you?

_____
_____
_____
_____
_____
_____

These next verses from 2 Corinthians tell me if we are in a war and we have weapons, we must have an enemy!

"For though we live in the world, we do not wage war as the world does. The weapons we fight with are not the weapons of the world. On the contrary, they have divine power to demolish strongholds. We demolish arguments and every pretension that sets itself up against the knowledge of God, and we take captive every thought to make it obedient to Christ." (2 Cor. 10:3-5)

Spiritual warfare is taking back the territory and coming into agreement with the good report, we can do it! We take back the land given to us—for us and our future generations. What feels like an attack is actually enemy resistance because you entered the territory where he has his couch and refrigerator! It is the place he has made his home. We initiate the conflict to assert the dominion and authority of God.

Discipline and self-control aren't enough to change spiritual atmospheres. A good example is the person addicted to alcohol or food. They can stop excess consumption through will power, but the heart will still be hurting and the enemy will still occupy a stronghold. No one can "white knuckle" their way to inner freedom.

Freedom isn't something we do; it must be who we are. This hits precisely at the core of our enemies attack —the opposition against our identity in Him. It was the source of doubt used against Eve, it was the source of temptation against Jesus in the wilderness, and it was the source of fear that pricked Thomas' orphan heart.

The lies we believe fortify the enemies stronghold. In the enemy's game there is no love, no mercy, and no forgiveness. He is a liar and the father of lies (John 8:44).

Look back over your answers from Chapter 2, ask Papa God if, because of what happened, were there any lies you believed.

#1 What happened?
_____
_____

#2 How I responded...
_____
_____
_____

#3 "Papa God, because of what happened, are there any lies I believed?
_____
_____
_____
_____
_____

#4 "Papa God, do I still need to protect myself by believing this lie?" _____

If *no*, pray, "*I ask you to forgive me for believing this lie and I come out of agreement and renounce the lie of* _____."

"*Papa, what is the truth?*" _____
_____
_____
_____

When you know the truth, the truth will set you free (John 8:32).

"Papa God, because of the lies, would You show me if there are there any vows, pledges, or promises I made to protect myself? Write what He shows you...

_____
_____
_____
_____
_____
_____
_____
_____
_____
_____
_____
_____
_____
_____
_____
_____
_____
_____
_____

"Is it safe for me to renounce these vows, pledges, or promises now?"

_____
_____
_____

Now, come out of agreement with the vow, pledge, or promise.

"Papa God, I take full responsibility for my ungodly and unholy vow, pledge or promise and I ask You to forgive me for the vow, pledge, or promise of_____.

I renounce the vow pledge, or promise AND

through the power of Your Blood, I come out of agreement with the vow, pledge, or promise of_____.

I receive Your forgiveness and mercy.

Now that I have given this to You,

do You have something for me in exchange?"

_____
_____
_____
_____
_____
_____
_____
_____

How do you feel now?

Next we will address the orphan spirit and allies.

Read John 14

Jesus discerned Thomas' insecurity and fear. In recognition of Thomas attitude, Jesus identifies an "orphan" spirit manifested in Thomas' fear of being left alone, unprotected, uncovered, rejected and abandoned.

The door to the orphan spirit is experienced when trauma breaks through the barriers of safety. Survival insists that something cover the gaping wound.

Now that you have forgiven, identified lies and broken soul ties, renounced vows, pledges and promises, it is time to get rid of the orphan spirit. It is time to renounce and come out of agreement with the lie that you have been left unprotected, uncovered, rejected and abandoned. The orphan spirit attacks identity by wanting you to believe you don't belong. However, the truth is that you do…

"For you did not receive a spirit that makes you a slave again to fear, but you have received the Spirit of sonship. And by him we cry, Abba Father. The Spirit himself testifies with our spirit that we are God's children." Romans 8:15,16

In what ways have you experienced an orphan spirit?

_____
_____
_____
_____
_____
_____
_____
_____

By coming out of agreement with the orphan spirit, you are allowing Papa God to claim you, to name you, to call you His own.

Are you ready to get rid of the orphan spirit? _____
If the answer is "yes," then pray…

"Papa God, I ask You to forgive me for agreeing with the orphan spirit. I renounce the orphan spirit that has lied to me that I am unprotected, uncovered, alone, abandoned, and have been left to find my own way. I come out of agreement with the lies of

_____

AND

I break* the power of the orphan spirit in the Name of Jesus."

"Papa, what is the truth?"

_____
_____
_____
_____
_____
_____
_____
_____
_____
_____
_____
_____
_____
_____

"Papa, do YOU claim me?" _____

"Do YOU have a new name for me?" _____

If "yes," what is it?
_____

So, how are you doing with all this?
_____
_____
_____
_____

Are you ready to get rid of the unloving spirit? _____

If the answer is "yes," then pray…

"Papa God, I ask You to forgive me for agreeing with an unloving spirit and denying myself the full extent of Your love. I renounce the unloving spirit that has lied to me that I am unlovable or unacceptable. I break* the lie that the Cross and Jesus Blood wasn't full proof of God's love for me and I break* the lie that I can't trust and love others. I come out of agreement with the lies and I break* the power of the unloving spirit in the Name of Jesus."

"Papa, what is the truth?"

_____
_____
_____
_____
_____
_____
_____
_____
_____
_____

Are you ready to get rid of the religious spirit? _____

If the answer is "yes," then pray…

"Papa God, I ask You to forgive me for agreeing with a religious spirit and denying myself the full extend of Jesus' Cross and Blood. I renounce the religious spirit that has lied to me that I need to control or manipulate and "do" in order to "be." I come out of agreement with the fear of trusting others and You.

I break* the lie that the Cross and Jesus Blood isn't sufficient to protect me. I come out of agreement with the lies and I break* the power of the religious spirit in the Name of Jesus."

"Papa, what is the truth?"

_____
_____
_____
_____
_____
_____
_____
_____
_____
_____
_____

Are you ready to get rid of the punishing spirit? _____

If the answer is "yes," then pray...

"Papa God, I ask You to forgive me for agreeing with a punishing spirit and denying myself Your full payment for my sins through Jesus' Cross and Blood. I renounce the punishing spirit that has lied to me that I have to continue to punish myself for the things Jesus died to give me.

I ask You to forgive me for believing the lie that I don't deserve the benefits of the Kingdom or any way I have denied myself the blessings, gifts, and destiny You have given me through Jesus resurrection..

I break* the lie that the Cross and Jesus Blood isn't sufficient to pay for all my sin and wrong doing. I come out of agreement with the lies and I break* the power of the punishing spirit in the Name of Jesus."

"Papa, what is the truth?"

_____
_____
_____
_____
_____
_____
_____
_____
_____
_____

Read John 14:17 and John 14:26

Do you want to experience the Holy Spirit? _____

If "yes," then pray…

"Papa God, I invite the Holy Spirit, the comforter and counselor, to fill me with His Presence. I come into agreement with the Spirit of Truth and receive the Truth of Your love, presence, and reality."

What is God showing you now?

___

Now, ask Papa to send you His Spirit of Adoption ...

___

What is He showing you?

___

Handling future thoughts...

Thoughts that linger and persist consume our productivity, demanding our attention. They are usually thoughts that strike a vulnerable or unresolved emotional area and become a trigger point.

When the thought is persistent, you don't know the source or can't resolve it, challenge it with the following process.

Is this condemnation or conviction?

Condemnation is from the enemy. It produces false guilt with spiritual death as a goal. It overshadows and points to mistakes or sin. Condemnation's motive is an invitation to resurrect the gravesite of your past, returning to relationship with the Old Music and Old Dances.

Conviction is from the Holy Spirit. It produces true guilt with holiness as a goal. It overshadows and points to mistakes or sin. Conviction's motive invites you to surrender the situation to the gravesite and return your focus on the resurrected Christ in you uniting in relationship with Him.

Is this temptation or a test?

Temptation is from the enemy. Its goal is sin and separation from God. The attractive package contains handcuffs. If you indulge, the attraction will turn to distraction and condemnation will scream accusations.

A test is from God. Its goal is Christian character and draws us closer to God. Tests are often lessons in stewardship. They don't always feel good but ultimately work for our good.

If the thoughts are about sins, behaviors, attitudes OR from protectors or lies that were surrendered and prayed through, you've asked for forgiveness and you have forgiven others, then stand firm, rejecting the lie.

_____
_____
_____

If you are not sure, pray about it immediately. Resolve the guilt by accepting any of your personal responsibility.

Ask and receive God's forgiveness.

_____
_____
_____

If it is something you are not responsible for, then place responsibility where it belongs then surrender and forgive.

Resist and stand firm, rejecting the lie.

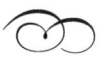

_____
_____
_____

Discerning the voice of the Good Shepherd is important. Jesus tells us that we will know His voice (John 10:14). Discernment protects you from receiving a false comforter or self-protective behavior which is a lie baited with pain, stress or fear, etc.

The voice of the Good Shepherd will always lead you. The voice of another will drive you. Refuse to follow the voice of "another." Allow the Spirit of Truth, who is in you, to keep your motives pure. Being tempted does not mean you are sinning. Remember, Jesus was tempted and refuted the lies with truth.

Learn your trigger points. What are the circumstances that cause you to lose your peace?

If you feel triggered, a key is to ask God to show you what He wants you to know about yourself and that situation. Then surrender, forgive and renounce any lies, receive His truth.

Revelation opens the door to access.

Read Matthew 14:35-36… what do these scriptures tell you?

_____
_____
_____
_____

__Praying__

For the balance of the weeks, center prayer time around those who did not apprehend the teaching or fully understand how to pray through the exercise.

__Helps__

The Bible says our enemy is called by different names. This partial list of names discloses characteristics of his personality. They help us identify his strategy that aims to attack the very core of our relationship with God.

- Accuser (Revelation 12:10)
- Adversary (I Peter 5:8)
- Angel of the Bottomless Pit (Revelation 9:11)
- Devil (Matthew 4:1)
- God of this World (II Corinthians 4:4)
- Father of Lies (John 8:44)
- Lucifer (Isaiah 14:12)
- Murderer (John 8:44)

- Prince of the Power of the Air (Ephesians 2:2)
- Prince of this World (John 14:30)
- Ruler of Darkness (Ephesians 6:12)
- Satan (Acts 5:3)
- Tempter (Matthew 4:3)
- Wicked One (Matthew 13:19)

Our Authority

We have a promise for security.

"Once you were alienated from God and were enemies in your minds because of your evil behavior. But now He has reconciled you by Christ's physical body through death to present you holy in His sight, without blemish or accusation — if you continue in your faith, established and firm, not moved from the hope held out in the Gospel," Colossians 1:21-23,

We have a promise for sonship (and daughtership!)

"...To all those who believed in His name, He gave the right to become children of God — children born not of natural descent, nor of human decision or a husband's will, but born of God," John 1:12-13,

We have a promise for service.

"I have given you authority to trample on snakes and scorpions and to overcome all the power of the enemy . . . ." Luke 10:19.

We have a promise forever.

"To him who overcomes, I will give the right to sit with Me on My throne, just as I overcame and sat down with My Father on His throne," Revelation 3:21.

Our Weapons

Jesus is out shield and our arrow.

Herod could not kill Him

Satan could not seduce Him

Death could not destroy Him

And the grave could not hold Him.

His Blood

- Jesus' blood is pure, (Leviticus 17:11)
- Jesus' blood is priceless, (I Peter 1:18-20
- Jesus' blood is powerful, (Revelation 12:11)
- Jesus' blood is preserved, (Hebrews 10:10)

His Name

- His name is pure, (Philippians 2:9)
- His name is priceless, (Isaiah 7:14)
- His name is powerful, (Philippians 2:10)
- His name is preserved, (John 14:6)

His Word

- His Word is pure, (Psalm 12:6)
- His Word is priceless, (John 1:1)
- His Word is powerful, (Hebrews 4:12)
- His Word is preserved, (I Peter 1:23)

Homework

- **Read Chapter 8 in Dancing on the Graves of Your Past book**
- **Complete Chapter 8 in Dancing on the Graves of Your Past workbook**

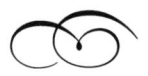

Handouts

Do you have any optional information or handouts for your group this week?

12

Week Nine
"Dance of the Kingdom"

"Now unto him who is able to do immeasurably more than all we ask or imagine..."
— Ephesians. 3:20

How to

Call the meeting to order with words of welcome and prayer. Be sure to use eye contact and acknowledge everyone. Allow light conversation but start on time.

Teaching

Dancing on the Graves of Your Past book

Book Chapter 8

DANCE OF THE KINGDOM

*"Now unto him who is able to do immeasurably
more than all we ask or imagine…"*
— Ephesians. 3:20

Imagine you are driving a car and spending all your time looking into the rear view mirrors, focusing on where you have been rather than looking ahead through the windshield to where you are going. It is safer and more productive to know where we are going. The past is a road mark which you have already passed by. It is a good reference point but a bad place to park the car!

God partnered with us in our past so we could partner with Him in our future. When you partner with God in the Dance of the Kingdom, you are fulfilling Paul's exhortation to leave our past behind and press on toward the higher calling in Jesus (Phil. 4:13,14). Partnering with God *is* taking our seat in Heavenly places with Christ Jesus (Eph. 2:6) with full access to our identity and inheritance in Jesus. When you move forward, the Holy Spirit clears the windshield so you can freely pay attention to your future and fulfill your destiny.

The surrendered, forgiven, overcoming heart following His lead can hear the things of God and realize He is releasing them into the realm of the impossible. In practical terms this means God didn't save, heal, and deliver you so you could just go to Heaven. He gave you a assignment—to demonstrate the will of God, here and now, through His radical power and presence.

The Divine purpose of dancing in the Kingdom is to demonstrate His Presence by answering people's hearts and prophesying their destiny.

God has not kept His mysteries a secret. He has not hid them from us but rather He has hid them *for* us (Prov. 25:2). Jesus' ministry was a model, a live demonstration. Jesus showed us how the Dance of the Kingdom works with His Papa as a partner. He did it through performing miracles, healing the sick, raising the dead, casting out demons, and cleansing the leper. Then Jesus made a profound statement that commissioned us to do the same (Matt: 10: 7,8). He told us we would do even do greater things. *"I tell you the truth, anyone who has faith in me will do what I have been doing. He will do even greater things than these, because I am going to the Father"* (John 14:12).

Have you prayed for someone who is sick and seen them healed? Have you prayed for someone who is tormented and seen them delivered? I have and there is nothing more gratifying than knowing we are plugged into the true source of love and power.

In a recent meeting I had a Word of Knowledge about scoliosis. Two ladies came forward for prayer. One had been in a severe auto accident many years earlier (trauma) and when we prayed her arm lengthened, the pain vanished and her spine straightened! The other lady had pain in her back and one leg was almost 1½ inches shorter than the other. We prayed and her leg lengthened and the back pain was gone!

When you begin this amazing Dance of the Kingdom it will awaken a desire for more and simultaneously require full dependency on God. Even Jesus said *"the Son can do nothing of Himself"* (John 5:19). So when God commissions us to do what Jesus did, we follow suit in knowing that we are incapable without the Father's help.

God is actually interested in your desires and dreams. Paul called it "co-laboring" with Christ (2Cor. 6:1), partnering in the work of Heaven. God's will co-laboring with man's will is seen in Genesis 2:19. God created the animals and then God gave Adam responsibility for naming them.

God didn't hang out and micro-manage Adam, give him hints or try to influence his decisions. God had full confidence in Adam's ability. Naming the animals was more significant than coming up with a word used to identify them. Naming the animals was assigning their character and nature. God created then Adam created. Together they displayed the model of co-laboring. Co-laboring with God means, with joined creativity, you can influence a fallen world. God is creative. He creates. It is who He is and what He does! He created man in His image and inherent in that image is the desire to create. When we create we are most like our Father. He created the original and we become imitators, illustrators of His nature, drawing attention to the true original.

All my life I was creative but creativity had been silenced and stolen by Old Music and Old Dances. The death of creativity is part of the enemies plan to destroy the desire to live and breathe outside the box of religion. I saw this first hand in the country of Russia. The people had lived so long under the strict Communist reign that when they were finally able to build free enterprise they didn't know how. They were bound and afraid and I heard many of them petition for the return of Communism that originally provided work and places to live. They wanted freedom but weren't willing to pay the price to keep it. Freedom will cost you something to embrace it, activate it, and then to give it away. It will require moving forward.

Desire, according to Proverbs 13:12, is a *"tree of life."* The revelation of co-laboring with God and discovering our ideas, talents, gifts and dreams are an expression of Him generates a desire and a passion for life. The element of co-laboring in creativity has become one of my passionate subjects!

In discussing creativity with a worship leader, he asked me to help one of the congregants. Apparently during worship the person would draw cartoons and the worship leader found this to be somewhat disrespectful and distracting. I watched to see what was happening. As if on cue, when worship began the cartoonist began drawing. The man's face and pencil moved with expression and flow. There was definitely something more going on. Later I explained that worship is a creative expression and the person was naturally expressing creativity, which is a form of worship. It was the person co-laboring in expressive adoration of our creator.

Wisdom is a creative craftsman, a co-laboring, Spirit of God according to these excerpts from Proverbs:

"The Lord brought me forth as the first of his works, before his deeds of old; I was appointed from eternity, from the beginning, before the world began.... Then I was the craftsman at his side. I was filled with delight day after day, rejoicing always in his presence...For whoever finds me finds life and receives favor from the Lord." (Prov. 8: 22-35)

I think it is pretty wild that Wisdom is the Creative Spirit of God. It opens the door to realize that co-laboring in creativity is more than artistic expression. Wisdom creates inventions, technology, governmental institutions, administrations, social systems, engineering, architecture, science, medical breakthroughs, and so on.

We expand the territory of God by releasing what He has given us and demonstrating who we are called to be, His friends. Jesus said, *"I no longer call you servants, because a servant does not know his master's business. Instead, I have called you friends, for everything that I learned from my Father I have made known to you"* (Jn. 15:15). We are God's friend. Friends talk, share, commune, laugh and cry together. They share dreams, ideas, and plan to spend time together. Friendship is greater than servanthood but it doesn't replace it. Friends are the greatest servants of all because they serve out of love not out of duty.

As friends of God, our inheritance of wisdom and creativity is to be released to the world. What would it be like to have ideas that would transform business, governments, or nations? What are your dreams, your desires? The answers to these two questions could beautifully merge to create a world changing influence.

Sometimes when we day dream or our mind wonders it is actually God taking us on a revelatory adventure. The co-laboring adventure may be for you or for someone else. It releases you into the prophetic—hearing from God for the people.

A young couple caught my attention and as I watched them I had thoughts that they were going to travel internationally. I felt as though they would carry a great influence where they went and would impact a people group. When I spoke this to them, they began to cry. They were both in law school studying international law. Their goal was to use international legal systems to rescue children from the slave trade. He used me to tell them He saw their dreams and desires and used revelation to prophesy

Receiving Kingdom revelation is not something you can muster up through good works or attending church. This is why surrender and forgiveness are so important. The Holy Spirit descended on the Lamb of God and remained giving Truth, Comfort and Counsel. *"And the Holy Spirit descended in bodily form like a dove upon Him, and a voice came from heaven which said, You are My beloved Son; in You I am well pleased"* (Luke 3:22). Tenderness of heart yielded in "son-ship" unlocks Gods mysteries and revelation is ushered in by the Holy Spirit.

The Dance of the Kingdom requires tuning in to His station. It is watching, listening, and moving with Him to display His power. When we purpose to focus on Him we find out He has great things to say! He is passionate about you and me. He has our picture on His refrigerator!

The road into the Kingdom of God is narrow as explained in Matt. 7:14, *"But small is the gate and narrow the road that leads to life, and only a few find it"*. However, once you are inside it is an adventure in *"righteousness, and peace, and joy in the Holy Ghost"* (Rom. 14:17). Life inside the Kingdom is an extraordinary partnership dance with Him! I really like the "joy" part!

Discussing

Experience the Journey Homework Review

Did they finish the homework?

How did they do with it…any trouble understanding the assignment?

What did they learn new?

Who would like to share?

Workbook Chapter 8

Dance of the Kingdom

"Now unto him who is able to do immeasurably more than all we ask or imagine..."
— Ephesians. 3:20

God partnered with us in our past so we could partner with Him in our future. When you partner with God in the Dance of the Kingdom, you are fulfilling Paul's exhortation to leave our past behind and press on toward the higher calling in Jesus (Phil. 4:13,14). Partnering with God is taking our seat in Heavenly places with Christ Jesus (Eph. 2:6) with full access to our identity and inheritance in Jesus.

Are you ready to accept your seat in Heavenly places with Papa?
_____

Pray and ask Papa to show you what your seat look like?
_____
_____
_____
_____
_____

The Divine purpose of dancing in the Kingdom is to demonstrate His Presence by answering people's hearts and prophesying their destiny. God is actually interested in your desires and dreams. Paul called it "co-laboring" with Christ.

Read 2 Cor. 6:1

What are your desires and dreams?
_____
_____
_____
_____
_____

God is creative. He creates. It is who He is and what He does! He created man in His image and inherent in that image is the desire to create. When we create we are most like our Father. He created the original and we become imitators, illustrators of His nature, drawing attention to the true original.

In what way are you an imitator of Him?

_____
_____
_____
_____

Read Proverbs 8:22-35

What do these verses tell you about Wisdom being the creative Spirit of God?

_____
_____
_____
_____
_____
_____
_____
_____

Wisdom is the craftsman that creates inventions, technology, governmental institutions, administrations, social systems, engineering, architecture, science, medical breakthroughs, and so on.

How does Wisdom speak to you?

_____
_____
_____
_____
_____
_____
_____

We expand the territory of God by releasing what He has given us and demonstrating who we are called to be, His friends. Jesus said, "I no longer call you servants, because a servant does not know his master's business. Instead, I have called you friends, for everything that I learned from my Father I have made known to you" (John 15:15). We are God's friend. Friends talk, share, commune, laugh and cry together. They share dreams, ideas, and plan to spend time together. Friendship is greater than servanthood but it doesn't replace it. Friends are the greatest servants of all because they serve out of love not out of duty.

How do you demonstrate your friendship with Jesus?

_____
_____

_____
_____
_____
_____
_____
_____
_____
_____
_____
_____
_____
_____
_____

As friends of God, our inheritance of wisdom and creativity is to be released to the world.

Ask Papa God right now... *"What ideas do You want to give me to transform business, governments, or nations?"*

_____
_____
_____
_____

Sometimes when we day dream or our mind wonders it is actually God taking us on a revelatory adventure. The co-laboring adventure may be for you or for someone else. It releases you into the prophetic—hearing from God for the people.

Do you hear from God on behalf of others? _____

What does that look like for you?

_____
_____
_____
_____

The Holy Spirit descended on the Lamb of God and remained giving Truth, Comfort and Counsel. Tenderness of heart yielded in "son-ship" unlocks Gods mysteries and revelation is ushered in by the Holy Spirit.

Ask Papa for a greater awareness of His Peace to you now…

_____
_____

Ask Papa to bring you the gift of Joy…

_____
_____

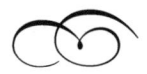

Praying

For the balance of the weeks, center prayer time around those who did not apprehend the teaching or fully understand how to pray through the exercise.

Helps

Talk about prophetic gifting but keep on track by sharing what you know about prophetic gifting.

Read Yvonne's book, Prophetic Gates, for a better understand of how prophetic gifts partner with creativity.

Homework

- Read Chapter 9 in Dancing on the Graves of Your Past book
- Complete Chapter 9 in Dancing on the Graves of Your Past workbook

13

Week Ten
"Dance Face to Face"

*"Come! Whoever is thirsty, let him come; and whoever wishes,
let him take the free gift of the water of life."*
—Revelation 22:17

How to

Call the meeting to order with words of welcome and prayer. This is your last week and everyone is usually very excited. I usually bring a card or have a prophetic word for each of them who completed the group.

Teaching

Dancing on the Graves of Your Past book

Chapter 9

Dance Face to Face

"Come! Whoever is thirsty, let him come; and whoever wishes, let him take the free gift of the water of life."
—Revelation 22:17

Spiritual hunger can be satisfied by one thing—His Presence. The intimacy of God's presence fulfills all desire. Haggai 2:7 speaks prophetically of the *"desire of all nations will come, and I will fill this house with glory."*

In the King James translation of Romans 8:19,22 Paul says the *"whole creation groaneth and travaileth in pain together until now"* Bible commentators Jamison, Fausset and Brown (Blue Letter Bible) add this amplification.

"It was enslaved, and the better self longed to be free; every motion of grace in the multitudinous heart of man was a longing for its Deliverer…every sigh from out of its manifold ills, were notes of the one varied cry, 'Come and help us.' Man's heart, formed in the image of God, could not but ache to be reformed by and for Him…"

Jesus fulfills the desire of man's longing. It isn't doing something for Him or Him doing something for you. It is *being* with Him without barriers. *"And we, who with unveiled faces all reflect the Lord's glory, are being transformed into his likeness with ever-increasing glory, which comes from the Lord, who is the Spirit."* (2 Cor. 3:18) It is our "unveiled face" that reflects His glory. Intimacy is transparency. One of our pastors at Bethel, Danny Silk, says intimacy can be defined as *"into me you see."*

Everything is to lead us into His embrace—the resting place of His Presence. The dance of a lifetime is the intimate Dance Face to Face. Being present with His Presence is a spiritual encounter with the King of Kings.

Kneeling at the foot of the Cross in prayer I experienced Jesus' Blood washing over me. In my spirit, I continued to look up toward Heaven acknowledging redemption and love. Instantly the Blood turned into streams of glitter, gold dust, jewels, colorful confetti, and flashes of light. I felt the Lord tell me these were gifts through His Blood and they were free. He said I could have as many as I want. Yes, I was greedy and began to reach for as many as I could grab hold of. I was having a great time focusing on all the presents from Him.

In the midst of my reaching I felt a hand touch mine. When I looked again, it was the hand of the Lord, taking hold of my hand. He began to lift me to my feet and bring me higher up, past the Blood, past the Cross, and past the Gifts. He brought me up to His Face and looked into my eyes. It was then I realized that the Blood, the Cross, the Gifts were all for this one moment…that I would see His Face. Nothing else matters. The presents were a means to get me to His presence, an intimate experience with Him.

My spiritual dad, Ernie Rogers, told me a story about news journalist and CBS anchorman, Walter Cronkite, who presented a commentary (1960's) on the Baptism in the Holy Ghost. Mr. Cronkite interviewed those who were filled with the Holy Spirit, manifested His Presence through bodily expression (Holy rollers), spoke in unknown tongues, and prayed with people, performing miracles, and the sick were healed. He confirmed they had a genuine experience. Mr. Cronkite also interviewed those who were against the indwelling of the Holy Spirit and speaking in unknown tongues. They gave their theological contentions, negated the fruit and effectiveness. The journalist confirmed they had a genuine argument.

Walter Cronkite reported both sides of the story. At the close of his presentation he said there were genuine experiences and genuine arguments. Then he said something like, I don't know about you, but I'd rather have an experience than an argument!

My last 4 years at Bethel Church has exposed me to the supernatural work of God. At first I had what I called "spiritual whiplash." I had never seen God move in miraculous power—blind eyes opened, deaf ears opened, broken bones healed, tumors disappeared, pain and infirmity gone, emotional breakthroughs, instant deliverance from depression and oppression.

In Mexico on a Bethel School of Ministry mission trip we encountered an 18 month old baby girl whose legs were twisted and curled. My friend, Kay, prayed for the baby and the baby's legs began to straighten.

By the end of the meeting the baby's legs were healed and she was learning to walk for the first time. Bethel Church keeps a testimony archive filled with stories of the miraculous.

Just as significant is the paradigm shift I experienced in God healing emotional distress and wounds. My earlier years of ministry included revelation and the prophetic but those gifts were always combating the popular emotional healing processes, programs, and recovery approaches. I still think maturity is a process but I see God moving more quickly and thoroughly in the arena of emotional breakthrough.

My first dentist appointment as a child was really bad. I had lots of cavities and the dentist had no patience. The dentist yelled at me and forced my hands on the chair arms while he worked on my teeth. I complied but was paralyzed with fear. All these years I have hated going to the dentist. I would spend so much time praying before and during appointments and tried all kinds of mental games to calm myself down. A few visits ago I was sitting in the dreaded chair, tears streaming down my face. Believe me, I have forgiven the dentist, the dental assistant, the dental office receptionist, my mom for taking me there and any one else associated with the dental industry!

This time I finally asked the Lord "What is up with this?" This time I waited for an answer! I closed my eyes and felt Him show me a picture of myself as that little girl terrified in the dentist chair. I saw the picture of Jesus sitting in the dentist chair and I was in His lap. His arms were wrapped around me and His hands were over mine on the chair arms. My small head rested back against His broad chest as the dentist worked on my teeth. I heard Him tell me was taking care of me that He gently held my hands down so I would be safe. Right after this experience I felt peace and His Presence. All the nervous shaking left my body and I actually felt calm. My current dentist completed the procedure that day and I felt no anxiety or discomfort. I have had other dentist visits since then and although it still isn't my favorite thing to do, I didn't feel nervous or fearful.

In the Transformation Center at Bethel Church where I am on Pastoral Counseling Staff, we see physical healing accompanying emotional healing. Through Bethel Sozo, and encounters with Him, people are emotionally healed and set free in one step!

Many times our physical body is the scene of the crime committed against us. We can hold in our body the residual effects of trauma. For example it can be common to see women who have been sexually abused continually struggle with bladder infections and painful menstrual cycles. When the power and presence of God comes and there is an emotional release we also press in for the physical healing and see mind, emotions and body healed.

Pastor Bill Johnson says any revelation from God's Word that doesn't lead us into an encounter with God only serves to make us more religious. The Church cannot afford 'form without power' for it creates Christians without purpose.

It is the Holy Spirit that brokers Heaven's encounters. He is available to those who follow in faith. Experiencing profound encounters with God should be part of the normal Christian life.

Knowing truth sets you free, but truth should lead us into revelation; the Kingdom realized. *"The kingdom of God is not in word but in power."* (1 Cor 4:14-20)

Kingdom power is inside of you in the form of the Holy Spirit as Jesus told us in Luke 17:21 *"For behold, the kingdom of God is within you."* Also, *"he will be with you forever"* (John 14:16). Then, in John 14:17, Jesus said the world cannot see or know Him, but we know Him *"for he lives with you and will be in you."*

Jesus, in John 14:17, used two examples of the Holy Spirit's presence—*with* us and *in* us. The Holy Spirit is both around us and in us signifying His presence both external and internal.

In my third year of Bethel School of Supernatural Ministry I interned with Bonnie Johnson. Accessing His Presence through the internal Kingdom of God is a passion of hers and she helped me to understand it better.

The external Kingdom is experienced when we enter into an atmosphere of worship or sit under the anointing of a leader and we are affected by the Presence of God around us. "Soaking" was the term used to describe lying down quietly and allowing the external atmospheric Presence of God to penetrate into our spirit. Think of grandma's pickling methods! The vegetables took on the taste and smell of the solution it soaked in.

When we learn to experience the internal Kingdom we access the "living water" Jesus gives so we will never be thirsty again (John 7:38). *"Whoever believes in me, as the Scripture has said, streams of living water will flow from within him."* Jesus told the Samaritan woman (John 4:10), *"If you knew the gift of God and who it is that asks you for a drink, you would have asked him and he would have given you living water."* Then Jesus tells her (vs. 38) for those who believe in Him, the same streams of living water would *"flow from within him."* The unending source of the Kingdom inside us goes with us wherever we go. It is accessible and available to be poured out to others.

He is both approachable and able to be captured. It is possible to position ourselves for an encounter with God. We do this by recognizing the signs of His presence. When He lifts the curtain of our senses to perceive Him, we have entered the Dance Face to Face.

Number 6:26-26 says, *"the Lord make His face shine upon you and be gracious to you."* In conjunction we are told in Matt: 5:16 *"In the same way, let your light shine before men, that they may see your good deeds and praise your Fa-*

ther in heaven." When God's face shines on our face, we become reflectors of His Glory to others. We have an encounter so we can be an encounter to others. It is the giving away of who we *are*.

"Then Mary took about a pint of pure nard, an expensive perfume; she poured it on Jesus' feet and wiped his feet with her hair. And the house was filled with the fragrance of the perfume." (John 12:3) It is most likely as Mary poured out the perfume it dripped or splashed on her hands, arms and clothing which probably offended the crowd even more! She didn't let the taunts and criticism stop her from pouring and smearing the perfume on Jesus allowing whatever overflow to inadvertently drip onto her. Interestingly, the word "Christ" means *anointed one* and is actually translated "to smear." When we press into Him and step past the religious spirit, we, too will be smeared with the anointing of the Holy Spirit. And the fragrant scent of His Presence will be a sign we have been with Him.

So, my friend, it's time to let go and forgive and move forward. The stage is set. Let the curtain of Heaven open. Put flowers on the graves and say *"goodbye."* He has arrived. Dance with Him. Dance on the graves of your past. Dance in His Kingdom, dance in His arms, dance while gazing into His face. Dance tenderly, dance in joy, dance wildly, dance with happy feet. Dance like no one is looking then dance for the world to see.

He is here... *"May I have this dance?"*

Discussing

Experience the Journey Homework Review

Did they finish the homework?

How did they do with it…any trouble understanding the assignment?

After writing their story,

>Were there any patterns they recognized?

>What did they learn new?

Who would like to share?

Workbook Chapter 9

Dance Face to Face

"Come! Whoever is thirsty, let him come; and whoever wishes, let him take the free gift of the water of life."
—Revelation 22:17

Read *Dancing on the Graves of Your Past*, Chapter 9 ~

Spiritual hunger can be satisfied by one thing—His Presence. The intimacy of God's presence fulfills all desire. Haggai 2:7 speaks prophetically of the "desire of all nations will come, and I will fill this house with glory."

Jesus fulfills the desire of man's longing. It isn't doing something for Him or Him doing something for you.

Read 2 Cor 3:18

It is being with Him without barriers. It is our "unveiled face" that reflects His glory.

Ask Papa to come now and reveal His Glory in your life...

_____
_____
_____
_____

Everything is to lead us into His embrace—the resting place of His Presence. The dance of a lifetime is the intimate Dance Face to Face. Being present with His Presence is a spiritual encounter with the King of Kings.

Many times our physical body is the scene of the crime committed against us. We can hold in our body the residual effects of trauma.

Ask Papa... "Do I have any physical issues connected with the trauma?"

_____
_____
_____
_____
_____
_____
_____

If "yes", put your hand on that area of your body and pray this...

"Papa, I ask You to forgive me for any way, known or unknown, that I caused my body to suffer for the emotional pain I have experienced."

With your hand on that area of your body, speak to your body...

"Body, I ask you to forgive me for making you perform past your limits. I ask you to forgive me for stressing you with bad habits. I ask you to forgive me for punishing you, hurting you or making you endure hardship."

"I come out of agreement with a spirit of trauma now in Jesus Name. I break* the spirit of trauma off my spirit, mind and my body. I come out of agreement with infirmity and break* it off my spirit mind and body now."

Try doing something you couldn't do before. For example, if your knee was stiff, try moving it...

What is happening now?

_____
_____
_____
_____
_____

Kingdom power is inside of you in the form of the Holy Spirit as Jesus told us in Luke 17:21 "For behold, the kingdom of God is within you."

Read John 14:17

What is God telling you about this verse?

_____
_____
_____
_____
_____

The Holy Spirit is both around us and in us signifying His presence both external and internal.

The external Kingdom is experienced when we enter into an atmosphere of worship or sit under the anointing of a leader and we are affected by the Presence of God around us. "Soaking" was the term used to describe lying down quietly and allowing the external atmospheric Presence of God to penetrate into our spirit.

When we learn to experience the internal Kingdom we access the "living water" Jesus gives so we will never be thirsty again. The unending source of the Kingdom inside us goes with us wherever we go. When He lifts the curtain of our senses to perceive Him, we have entered the Dance, Face to Face.

This is an exercise to access the internal Kingdom of God.

Read Psalm 16

Pick a verse you like. Which one did you pick? _____

Ok, now you are going to use that verse to access the Kingdom.

This is not an empting of your mind like some new age ritual...this is using your mind to access Him. We actually make our mind focus on what our spirit is connecting with, rather than letting our mind run around like a 2 yr old causing chaos everywhere it ventures!

So you begin to focus on the scripture and press in...meaning you stay focused and concentrated on the verse...this allows the Holy Spirit to meet you and bring you into the Kingdom...accessing Heaven in YOU!

If your mind wanders, bring it back into focus with the scripture, repeat the scripture and force your mind to stay at task by letting your spirit be in charge. Keep doing this until your spirit can stay focused on the connection with the Kingdom. He will lead you into an encounter with His Presence IN YOU!

What is happening when you experience the connection with His Kingdom in you?

_____
_____
_____

"Then Mary took about a pint of pure nard, an expensive perfume; she poured it on Jesus' feet and wiped his feet with her hair. And the house was filled with the fragrance of the perfume" (John 12:3). It is most likely as Mary poured out the perfume it dripped or splashed on her hands, arms and clothing which probably offended the crowd even more! She didn't let the taunts and criticism stop her from pouring and smearing the perfume on Jesus allowing whatever overflow to inadvertently drip onto her. Interestingly, the word "Christ" means *anointed one* and is actually translated *"to smear."* When we press in and step pass the religious spirit, we, too will be smeared with the anointing of the Holy Spirit. And the fragrant scent of His Presence will be a sign we have been with Him.

So, my friend, put flowers on the graves of your past and say "goodbye." The world is your stage. Let the curtain of heaven open. He has arrived. Dance with Him. Dance on the graves of your past. Dance in His Kingdom, dance in His arms, dance while gazing into His face. Dance tenderly, dance in joy, dance wildly, dance with happy feet. Dance like no one is looking then dance for the world to see.

He is here… "May I have this dance?"

Go ahead, dance with Him! Write your experience…

_____
_____
_____
_____
_____

"…as the movement grew yet swifter, the interweaving yet more ecstatic, the relevance of all to all yet more intense, as dimension was added to dimension and that part of him which could reason and remember was dropped farther and farther behind that part of him which saw, even then, at the very zenith of complexity, complexity was eaten up and faded, as a thin white cloud fades into the hard blue burning of the sky, and a simplicity beyond all comprehension, ancient and young as spring, illimitable, pellucid, drew him with cords of infinite desire into its own stillness. He went up into such a quietness, a privacy, and a freshness that at the very moment when he stood farthest from our ordinary mode of being he had the sense of stripping off encumbrances and awaking from trance, and coming to himself."

C.S. Lewis, Perelandra, excerpt from pp. 218-219

Praying

Ask for volunteers who want to go over any of the previous lessons and pray through an issue. For the balance of the weeks, center prayer time around those who did not apprehend the teaching or fully understand how to pray through the exercise.

Helps

Ask everyone to share their dreams and goals.

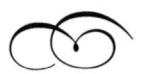

Homework

Finished!

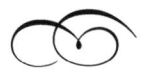

Handouts

Now is the time to ask if members want to commit to attending another group.

If so, ask them to fill out new <u>Participation Form.</u>

Leader's

Fill out the Leader's Evaluation (in Forms section) and discuss it with your mentor or leader.

14

Handling Conflicts and Difficult People

"And when the people of that place recognized Jesus, they sent word to all the surrounding country. People brought all their sick to Him and begged Him to let the sick touch the edge of His cloak, and all who touched Him were healed."
—Matthew 14:35-36

I planned the group, gathered information for teaching, neatly printed the handouts and bathed each step in prayer. What I did not plan for was the hurting personalities in my group that could dominate, or worse yet, attempt to destroy the group. I learned, often the hard way, certain personalities and conflicts within the group were destructive to the group as a whole. If allowed to continue, they could further wound the people in the group.

Remember, difficult people are hurting people. Their symptoms are exhibited as protectors and barriers. They are showing you, by their behavior, that they are still "stuck."

The following "red flags" are listed to prepare you to handle the most common conflicts and difficult situations.

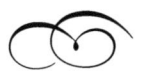

Too much talking.
Monopolizes time with tedious details.
Never gets to the point of the topic.
Interrupts and draws attention from others.
Is thinking about what to say while others talk.

- **Suggestions**

A. Reinforce that communication is talking AND listening; everyone needs time for both.

B. Summarize the point for them, then move on by saying something like, "Let's hear how someone else feels."

C. If all else fails, gently and lovingly confront the talker(s) about monopolizing the group's time.

D. You may suggest the talker(s) seek individual counseling if they need more than the group provides.

E. Set specific limits on discussion time and use a clock or timing device to limit talking time.

Too little talking.
Does not participate in discussions or share.
Frustration or fear that words will not come out right.

- **Suggestions**

A. Their silence could be fear or a lack of trust; allow time for them to feel safe enough to share.

B. Lovingly direct questions their way. For instance, "Have you ever felt like that?"

Too much emotion.

Seems unable to regain composure when crying or laughing.

Expresses feelings in destructive ways toward the group, leader, or themselves.

Uses emotional outbursts to control the group's direction.

- **Suggestions**

A. Allow the Holy Spirit's gift of discernment to help you determine when behavior is appropriate.

B. Use your authority to gain control; establish eye contact and speak to them lovingly but firmly about their emotions.

C. In order to protect the group, you may need to ask them to step outside the room. It the problem continues and is disruptive to the group on a weekly basis, you will need to pray about asking them not to return to the group. Refer to the section in this chapter on "Leaving the Group".

Too little emotion.

Appears unaffected when group members display emotion.

Distant and emotionally indifferent.

Talks from a thinking position rather than sharing feelings.

Observes rather than participates.

- **Suggestions**

A. Reinforce that the group benefits when everyone contributes.

B. Encourage that denying feelings only exaggerates the problem.

C. Direct questions to the heart, not the head. For example, "I'm wondering how you FEEL about that?" rather than asking what the person THINKS.

Too many presenting issues.

Scatters the group by jumping from one story to another without coming to the point.

Pulls attention from the group unity toward unrelated issues.

Sensationalizes or dramatizes stories.

- **Suggestions**

A. Reestablish the purpose for the group and welcome issues within that perimeter.

B. Gain control of wayward stories by rephrasing what you feel they are trying to say.

C. Simply state that time is running out and the group needs to hear what others need to share.

D. Set specific limits on discussion time.

E. Suggest individual counseling.

No presenting issues.
Does not identify with discussion topics.
Already dealt with "that" problem.
Desires to help others in the group without self-exposure.

- **Suggestions**

A. Restate the purpose of the group

B. Emphasize the group is there for those who are willing to look at their own issues

C. Look for ways to draw out their FEELINGS in discussions

Has all the answers.

Has solution, rebuttal, or advice for every person sharing.

Takes away attention from the person speaking.

Emphasizes how "they" handled a similar problem.

May battle leader for control of group and discussion.

- **Suggestions**

A. Regain control by not allowing interruptions

B. Lovingly confront the comments with, "I'd like to hear how the group feels about what you said."

C. Confirm that the group has a leader and everyone needs to be working on their own issues.

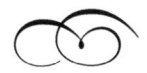

Has no answers.

Does not assume any responsibility for choices.

Makes no attempt to participate in their healing.

Deflects any help with "that won't work because" or "that's fine, but…"

Depressed and satisfied to stay in self-pity.

- **Suggestions**

A. Be compassionate but do not reinforce self-pity.

B. Confront apathy.

C. Accept that this person is not able or ready to change and/or deal with problems.

"Hyper" faith

Freely uses religious cliches or scriptures as confrontation or condemnation, rather than for encouragement.

Even deeply expressed emotional discussions end with statements like, "well, praise God anyway!"

Their religious activity seems to be a Band-Aid that covers real feelings.

- **Suggestions**

A. Confirm that the group is dedicated to following God and His Word. However even David in the Psalms cried out to God with fear, doubt and emotional confusion or pain.

B. Emphasize that our need, not our self-sufficiency, is why Christ died for us.

No faith.

Inability to trust God or the group.

Undermines the faith or trust that others express.

Brings to the group their ideas that are contrary to the culture of the group.

Does not attend church services or isn't in fellowship.

- **Suggestions**

A. Reestablish this is a Christian group following Biblical principles.

B. Research and correct teachings that do not align with the Bible or Biblical concepts.

C. If a person is not cooperating with the group in its foundational beliefs, they will be a source of division and distraction.

D. Suggest they move into individual counseling.

Contact From Group Members Outside the Group Setting

When you are contacted by group members outside the group setting, refrain from counseling them with regard to group matters. Ask them to save the comments or concerns for group time. If you do counsel someone outside the group about group conflicts and group issues, you will be allowing division within the group. It could even appear this person has special privileges or that you favor them by giving them more of your time.

If you are contacted by a friend/spouse of a group member, you must be careful not to break the confidence of the member. I thank the person for being concerned but refer any questions back to the group member to answer. I let the group member know this person called and said I referred the caller back to them.

I hold to these perimeters even if one of the group members is seeing me for individual counseling.

The quickest way to lose the trust and confidence of the group is to discuss the group or its members with anyone but your advisor.

Recognizing Your Limitations

Being prepared to handle crises is important for leadership. You may need to intervene with group members or their families. I will often receive a crisis call from someone who never met me but was given my number by a group member or their family. Your Resource List should contain contact information for the following local or regional community services:

- Suicide Prevention
- Food and Housing
- Mental Health
- Health or Dental Clinics
- Crises Shelters
- Protective Services for Youth/Elderly
- Education
- Counseling (preferably Christian focused)
- Financial
- Legal Help
- Child Care
- Rehabilitation Resources
- Transportation
- Hospitalization

Reporting Child or Elderly Abuse

It is your responsibility to educate yourself as to the reporting requirements of your state or region. Start by contacting your local Child Protective Agency for more information and to find out the protocol of abuse reporting. Ask them to send you hard copy blank forms in the event you need to report child or elder abuse.

Suicide Prevention

In addition, you should familiarize yourself with what to do in the event of a suicide threat or attempt. You probably will not receive this type of call frequently, but just one handled carelessly could be disastrous.

The following information is taken from Techniques in Crisis Intervention: A Training Manual by Farberow, Heilig, Litman, (SPCLA, 1968).

I include only a BRIEF synopsis of procedure for the handling of a potential suicide. This is a complex and life-threatening situation which requires qualified and extensive training. Sometimes local crises hotlines offer suicide prevention training courses. Do some research on your own so you feel well aware of what to do in the event of a suicide threat or attempt.

- Try to keep the person on the phone.
- Assure the person he did the right thing by calling.

- Write down their name, phone number, address, and information about the attempt.

- Question specifically what the person has ingested or what he/she has done or is doing.

- Call the police, identify yourself, and give them all the pertinent information for investigation.

-

Being Prepared

Occasionally, even with careful prescreening, I have run into extreme, disruptive problems. One such person was an undisclosed epileptic who had seizures when she addressed her abuse. The entire group was in a panic to hold her down and secure medical attention. As a result, some members ran screaming from the room and never came back to the group believing she had a demonic manifestation.

Other times, there have been members on medication due to psychological disorders. Their unpredictable personality patterns were hard for most members to handle.

Extreme behavior or severe personality changes require qualified or professional attention. Protecting the group from abusive behavior is essential. People who display extreme or disruptive behavior should be asked to leave the group and be referred to a pastor or professional Christian counselor qualified to help them. Behaviors to be aware of may include:

- Anger or aggression toward you or the group

- Chronic drug, alcohol or addictive acting out behaviors
- Extreme high's and low's
- Extreme change in personality
- Regressing in personality to a time of induced trauma
- Memories surfacing for the first time
- Occult activity

Any obviously non-normal behavior should be responded to in a timely manner. This is for your protection, the group's protection, and to protect the person in question.

These types of situations are not the usual, thank God! However, I have shared them in effort to make you aware. The best advice I can give is to admit when a situation is more than you bargained for and refer to someone equipped to minister to these behaviors.

Leaving the Group

A person may want to leave the group before his commitment is completed. Usually it is because they were not prepared to deal with the feelings that surfaced or because the group is not what was expected.

I try to encourage everyone to fulfill their commitment, but if they are determined to discontinue, I ask them to attend one more time and tell the group how they feel. This diminishes feelings of betrayal or abandonment by those who remain in the group.

If the person leaves the group and you need to let the group know, be brief but honest. Allow the group to express their feelings about the person leaving. The group may want to send a card expressing their sentiments of good-bye.

Sometimes someone leaves the group in anger or because you have asked him to leave. I briefly address this with the group personally and invite their feelings or comments.

In Conclusion

No matter what type of group you choose, there are going to be conflicts to challenge you. Prescreening helps to eliminate some problems but does not always guarantee harmony and unity within the group. If you are running open groups, you are more likely to find an array of personalities that may not gel. The good news is that the conflicts will help you learn to communicate more skillfully and be a better leader. This is one sure way of your growing closer to God! You have been placed in these lives for a season to help clear their cloudy windshield and God has the ultimate responsibility to change hearts and lives. It is good to leave the big stuff to Him.

Pray and ask God to give you His eyes, His ears, and a deeper love for those in your groups. He can give you rich insight into people's motives;

reveal prophetic insight and direction; give you a blessing where there was a mess.

Hurting people are often rejected because of their demanding attitudes. Your ability to handle the situation with compassion and love will be seen and felt by the other members. Their trust in you, the group, and God, flourishes as a result of your words being like apples of gold on platters of silver.

Jesus ministered with one goal only, and that was to bring glory to His Father. We cannot go wrong following His example.

15

The End is a Beginning

I tell you, open your eyes and look at the fields! They are ripe for harvest..."

—John 4:28-35

I have presented you with a practical guide to encourage you to begin and build a support group ministry. I want you to use the information like you would a basic recipe. As your confidence and experience grows, you can change, add, or customize your format to fulfill your goals and objectives.

What is important is that you do what God is calling you to do. Our God is creative and has given each of us different testimonies and different avenues to share with others. Your group ministry should be a reflection of your obedience to Him.

It isn't recorded whether Jesus ever got the drink of water He asked for from the Samaritan woman that day at the well. His purpose wasn't to satisfy His thirst but to fill her emptiness. "My food," said Jesus, "is to do the will of Him who sent Me and to finish His work. Do you not say, 'Four months more and then the harvest?' I tell you, open your eyes and look at the fields! They are ripe for harvest," (John 4:28-35, NIV).

The woman from Samaria dropped her water jug beside the well and ran toward town crying, "Come see the man ..."

Jesus was satisfied, watching His Father's glory being poured out through her.

God is still waiting at the well in your town; to meet you, heal you, and send you forth. Your inspiration to reach out to the hurting is evidenced by your willingness to read through this book. Let Jesus transform His vision into a reality through you. You don't need eloquent speeches or certificates. You just give what He gives you.

Will you take your tragedy and let Jesus make it a triumph?
Will you take your misery and let Jesus make it a ministry?
Will you take your past and let Jesus make it a present?

Then the people of Samaria said to the woman, "We no longer believe just because of what you said; now we have heard for ourselves, and we know that this man really is the Savior of the world."

—John 4:42

Appendix

Group Forms & Handouts

Dancing on the Graves of Your Past ~ Support Group Leader's Guide

Organization Worksheet

Your Name: _____

Date _____

Vision for this group:

_____
_____
_____

Type of group:

_____

Meeting Place:

_____

Address:

_____

How long will you be able to use this location? _____

Group will meet on _____ (day of week)

Time: from _____ to _____

How many weeks? _____

Group leader: _____   **Co-leader:** _____

    Address: _____   Address: _____

    Telephone: _____   Telephone: _____

    Email: _____   Email: _____

What format will you use?
_____

Will you allow cross-talk? _____

Will your group be open or closed? _____

Will you screen applicants? _____

    If "yes", how?
_____
_____
_____

What forms have you decided to utilize?

    1. _____
    2. _____
    3. _____
    4. _____
    5. _____
    6. _____

Is your group appropriate for men and women together? _____

If "yes", how will you handle gender conflicts? _____

To what age member(s) are you reaching out? _____

Are you a mandated reporter of abuse? _____

Will you need a "waiver of confidentiality" form? _____

    If "yes", attach a sample of the waiver.

Has your staff leader approved the waiver you will use? _____

How will you advertise for your group participants?
_____
_____

Who will be your group mentor or advisor?

    Name: _____

    Address: _____

    Telephone: _____ Email: _____

What information will your resource list contain?
_____
_____
_____
_____
_____
_____
_____

Will you chare for the group? ____ If "yes", how much? _____

Itemize your estimated expenses per group:

How will your expenses be paid?
_____

What additional concerns or details should you check into?
_____
_____

Week # _____

1. **How To**

    A. Teaching

    B. Discussing

    C. Praying

2. **Helps**

3. **Homework**

4. **Handouts**

Dancing on the Graves of Your Past ~ Support Group Leader's Guide

Participant Acknowledgment

Date:

Name:

Address:

City: Zip:

Telephone Number: Home: Email:

                       Cell:

What is the best time to reach you?

Single: Married: Divorced: Widowed: Other:

Who can we call in case of an emergency?

Name:

Address:

Telephone: Email:

Concerning Confidentiality:

   The undersigned understands that his/her case may be shared with (your church name) staff and/or leadership. The purpose of the discussion is to allow the staff to pray together about your concerns and to help one another understand and serve you in the most effective manner.

   In cases of the abuse of children or elderly, or corporal harm to another or yourself, we are legally bound by the state of (your state's name) to notify the proper authorities.

(initial) _____

Date group begins: _____

Our group will meet on _____ to _____ for _____ weeks.

Will you commit to attend each week and be on time? _____

Will you be faithful to complete homework assignments? _____

What problems are you experiencing? (Use additional paper if needed)

_____
_____

Why do you want to come to a support group?

_____
_____

Have you (now or sometime previously) received other ministry? ____

    If "yes", what type of ministry have you receive?

_____
_____

What Christian activities do you attend on a regular basis?

    How do you rate your relationship with Jesus?

    Excellent 10 9 8 7 6 5 4 3 2 1 None

How did you find out about our group or who referred you?

_____

Signature: _____ Date: _____

Welcome

Welcome to our support group. The purpose of this ministry is to offer love, encouragement and ministry to you. How you got where you are is not always as important as what you are doing with your pain now. What is going on in your heart, especially in your relationship with Jesus and others?

It is my prayer as you lean on Jesus to help you, that He will reveal Himself to you in a way you never knew possible. Today does not have to be yesterday's prison. It is only through Jesus and the power of the Holy Spirit we can be emotionally free.

This process may seem like a roller coaster ride. Feelings will mount high and then seem to plunge to the ground. However, just like the roller coaster, be encouraged that you are moving forward! Trust is an area we are all challenged, but remember, you will get from the group what you are wiling to emotionally invest into it.

Please be sure to take your time filling out all the forms. This information will help me know more about your specific needs and how to help the group as a whole. Thank you for answering His challenge to grow in Him.

Letter to My Family

I am giving you this letter to let you know that I will be attending a support group for Christians who are hurting emotionally. The purpose of the group is not to blame others for my problems or to talk about anyone else. It is to help me deal with my personal issues and how I feel. The support group will help me find hope, strength, and healing for some very painful emotional issues I have been dealing with lately.

I am told that addressing these unresolved areas in my life could cause me to feel a variety of emotions including depression or anger. I want you to know I will try my best not to take these emotions out on you or the family. There may be times I need to cry or want to be alone. Please don't feel this has anything to do with my love or feelings for you.

I may not always be able to express or acknowledge what is going on inside me but that doesn't mean I am not making progress. You can help me through this time by being willing to listen to me when I need to talk or by giving me quiet time when I feel overwhelmed.

Our relationship has already been affected by my unresolved problems and because I care for you and our relationship, I am willing to do what I can in order to make it better. I realize you may not understand all the reasons why I feel I need a support group but it is important for me to have your blessings and encouragement. I feel it is God's timing for me to work toward reconciliation and peace with my past, my family, and my relationship with God.

Dancing on the Graves of Your Past ~ Support Group Leader's Guide

Name and Contact Exchange

Group:

Leader's name: Email:

Co-leader's name: Email:

Member's name: **Email:**   **Phone:**

1.
2.
3.
4.
5.
6.
7.
8.
9.
10.
11.
12.
13.

Dancing on the Graves of Your Past Support Group Guidelines

Welcome to our support group. The purpose of our group is to offer love, encouragement, and ministry. How you got where you are is not always as important as what you are doing with the pain now What is going on in your heart?

It is my prayer as you lean on Jesus and the Holy Spirit to help you, He will reveal Himself to you in a new way. Today does not have to be yesterday's prison. You can be emotionally free. You can experience joy and dance on the graves of your past.

The emotional healing process can seem like a roller coaster ride. Feelings will mount high then seem to drop low. But you ARE moving forward! Trust is an area we are all challenged, but you will get from the group what you are willing to invest into your time and commitment to your healing. You can choose your level of participation.

Within the group there are guidelines and a few rules:

- **No cross-talk** (use "I" statements)
- **No judging** (avoid comments that condemn or criticize)
- **No advice-giving** (no preaching or telling someone what they should do)
- **No interruptions** (allow someone their talking, crying, or being angry)
- **No spiritualizing or analyzing** (feelings require a response not intellect)
- **No gossip** (we are here to work on our own problems)

Confidentiality is important. You have been ask to refrain from talking about anyone outside the group setting. This protects and honors everyone. It is the facilitator's job to limit or stop inappropriate conversations.

Group Leader _____

Healthy Support Groups

1. WE BUILD TRUST THROUGH CONFIDENTIALITY

In keeping with Christian integrity, there should be no violation or breach of confidentiality. Refrain from gossip, both in and outside the group meeting. Gossip is defined here as any discussion of or about other group members, without their being present, which is positive or negative, no matter what the intended purpose.

2. WE RESPECT OTHERS' BOUNDARIES
(Spiritual, Emotional, and Physical)

Respect others' needs by asking what they would feel comfortable receiving. It is important to use discretion and express affection in a manner appropriate for the individual.

3. WE GIVE AND RECEIVE SUPPORT AND ENCOURAGEMENT

When we come together as a group, we can comfort each other, as we have been comforted by God. To support other people is not to give them advice or try to rescue them. If we are struggling with a problem, we can find at least one other person who has worked through a similar struggle. That person is often the one best equipped to minister to those striving to overcome similar problems without giving advice.

4. WHEN WE SHARE. WE FOCUS ON OUR FEELINGS

We avoid intellectualizing and spiritualizing. We refrain from trying to "explain" situations when sharing, and do our best to clearly identify and share our feelings. Feelings do not require analysis; they require proper response. As we progress in this work, appropriate labels for feelings develop, (such as joy, fear, peace, sadness, depression, anger, love, resentment, guilt, loneliness, and fulfillment).

5. WE RECOGNIZE THAT THE HOLY SPIRIT IS IN CHARGE

Realize that the leader is simply facilitating the group. We pray for guidance and direction, and ask the Holy Spirit to be present within each of us.

6. WE LIMIT OUR TALKING AND ALLOW OTHERS TO SHARE

Allow everyone in the group to have an equal opportunity to share. We talk about our own experience, strength, and hope without giving a full-length autobiography. We take turns talking and do not interrupt each other.

Journal Exercise A

Write about you doubts and fears about your identity then find a scripture that is truth.

How you feel~	What does God say ~
I feel like God never hears my prayers.	*"The eyes of the Lord are on the righteous and His ears are attentive to their cry."* **Psalm 34:12 (NIV)**

Journal Exercise B

Write about you doubts and fears about yourself then find a scripture that is truth.

How you feel~	What does God say ~
I feel alone	*"I will never leave you or forsake you."* *Hebrews 13:5 (NIV).*

Journal Exercise C

Acknowledging Old Music

True peace comes from being cleansed through repentance by God's grace and forgiveness. Read all the fifth chapter of Galatians and then begin the exercise.

1. Go through chapter 5, paying particular attention to verses 19-23. Make a list of any area in which you struggle.
2. For each sinful attitude or behavior, ask God to show how it has affected you or your relationships. Write down what is revealed to you.
3. Determine to take responsibility and resolve to change.
4. Ask for God's forgiveness. Read Psalm 51:1-2 and the handout entitled <u>God's Promises on Forgiveness.</u>
5. Make a commitment, in the strength of god, to sin no more in that way.
6. Accept His forgiveness.
7. Praise and thank god for His faithfulness.
8. Re-read Galatians 5:1, "It is for freedom that Christ has set us free. Stand firm, then, and do not let yourselves be burdened again by a yoke of slavery." (NIV).

Journal Exercise D

Promises I Can't Afford To Keep

"If any of you lacks wisdom, he should as God, who gives generously to all without finding fault, and it will be given to him," James 1:5 (NIV).

Pray and ask for God's wisdom in your life. Review your journal and homework from the past few weeks. Have you made promises to yourself as a result of past experiences that keep you from intimacy in relationships, especially in your relationship with God?

What are they?

_____
_____
_____
_____
_____

What to you need to let go of?

_____
_____
_____

What do you need to hang on to?

Journal Exercise E

Practicing Forgiveness

The surrendered heart no longer wants the excess baggage of unforgiveness. Forgiveness, then, becomes a welcomed practice. Complete the following sentences.

Resisting Forgiveness

    I will forgive _____ if _____

Re-read the parable in Matthew 18:21-35.

    From what debt have you been released?
    _____

    Who is the servant you are holding in judgment?
    _____

Giving Forgiveness

    Father, I forgive _____ for _____.

    Father, I ask You to forgive me for blaming You for
    _____.

Asking Forgiveness

I am sorry for what I have done. Father, forgive me for
_____.

Receiving Forgiveness

Father, I receive Your forgiveness for
_____.

Father, I forgive myself for
_____.

Concluding Prayer

"Father, I bring You all my secrets and all my sins. I surrender my heart to You. I will no longer seek for acceptance from anyone but You. I will no longer seek for approval from anyone but You. I will no longer punish myself for those things for which You have forgiven me. I commit my life to loving. Papa God, thank You... Amen."

If needed…

Father, help me go to _____ and ask for their forgiveness. (If this person has already died, asking God for forgiveness is sufficient. It is unscriptural to pray to or try to communicate with anyone who is deceased.)

Journal Exercise F

Handling Thoughts

If you are experiencing thoughts and feelings that are disturbing your prayer life or productivity, write a detailed description of what is occurring. As you write, ask God to show you the source (whether it is conviction, condemnation, temptation, or trial).

_____
_____
_____
_____
_____
_____
_____

Apply the teaching to your situation. How will you take a stand?

_____
_____
_____
_____

Prayer

"Father, though we live in the world, we do not wage war as the world does. You have given us Jesus' blood, His name, and Your Word, the armor and prayer – our mighty weapons. These weapons have divine power, Your power, to demolish any stronghold of doubt, deception, or delusion."

"Right now, I use these weapons of truth to demolish arguments and pretensions:"

1.
2.
3.
4.

"These have set themselves against You and I confess I once accepted them. I take those thoughts captive by repenting and renouncing their validity. I make them obedient to Christ by submitting to the truth in Your Word that says:" (List scriptures that best reflects your affirmation.)

1.
2.
3.
4.

"Papa, what is the lie I believe?

_____
_____
_____

I come out of agreement with the lie and break any vow, promise or pledge that would hold me captive.

I believe I have Your Holy Spirit who promises to guide me into all truth."

"Papa God, what is the truth?

_____
_____
_____
_____
_____
_____
_____

Ephesians Chapter 1

Eph 1:1 Paul, an apostle of Christ Jesus by the will of God, To the saints in Ephesus, the faithful in Christ Jesus:

Eph 1:2 Grace and peace to you from God our Father and the Lord Jesus Christ.

Eph 1:3 Praise be to the God and Father of our Lord Jesus Christ, who has blessed us in the heavenly realms with every spiritual blessing in Christ.

Eph 1:4 For he chose us in him before the creation of the world to be holy and blameless in his sight. In love

Eph 1:5 he predestined us to be adopted as his sons through Jesus Christ, in accordance with his pleasure and will-

Eph 1:6 to the praise of his glorious grace, which he has freely given us in the One he loves.

Eph 1:7 In him we have redemption through his blood, the forgiveness of sins, in accordance with the riches of God's grace

Eph 1:8 that he lavished on us with all wisdom and understanding.

Eph 1:9 And he made known to us the mystery of his will according to his good pleasure, which he purposed in Christ,

Eph 1:10 to be put into effect when the times will have reached their fulfillment-to bring all things in heaven and on earth together under one head, even Christ.

Eph 1:11 In him we were also chosen, having been predestined according to the plan of him who works out everything in conformity with the purpose of his will,

Eph 1:12 in order that we, who were the first to hope in Christ, might be for the praise of his glory.

Ephesians Chapter 1 (continued)

Eph 1:13 And you also were included in Christ when you heard the word of truth, the gospel of your salvation. Having believed, you were marked in him with a seal, the promised Holy Spirit,

Eph 1:14 who is a deposit guaranteeing our inheritance until the redemption of those who are God's possession-to the praise of his glory.

Eph 1:15 For this reason, ever since I heard about your faith in the Lord Jesus and your love for all the saints,

Eph 1:16 I have not stopped giving thanks for you, remembering you in my prayers.

Eph 1:17 I keep asking that the God of our Lord Jesus Christ, the glorious Father, may give you the Spirit of wisdom and revelation, so that you may know him better.

Eph 1:18 I pray also that the eyes of your heart may be enlightened in order that you may know the hope to which he has called you, the riches of his glorious inheritance in the saints,

Eph 1:19 and his incomparably great power for us who believe. That power is like the working of his mighty strength,

Eph 1:20 which he exerted in Christ when he raised him from the dead and seated him at his right hand in the heavenly realms,

Eph 1:21 far above all rule and authority, power and dominion, and every title that can be given, not only in the present age but also in the one to come.

Eph 1:22 And God placed all things under his feet and appointed him to be head over everything for the church,

Eph 1:23 which is his body, the fullness of him who fills everything in every way.

Reread the chapter and circle all the benefits of being an heir to the Kingdom of God!

Dancing on the Graves of Your Past ~ Support Group Leader's Guide

NOT-TO-BE-MAILED LETTER

To _____

(or, if person has died) To _____ c/o Papa God

This is what you did…

_____
_____
_____
_____

You hurt me when you…

_____
_____
_____
_____

This is how it made me feel…

_____
_____
_____
_____

You are responsible for…

_____
_____
_____
_____

Your Name _____ Date _____

GOD'S PROMISES ON FORGIVENESS

"Blessed are they whose transgressions are forgiven, whose sins are covered. Blessed is the man whose sin the Lord will never count against him," Psalm 32:1-2.

"When we were overwhelmed by sins, You forgave our transgressions," Psalm 65:3.

"The Lord . . . who forgives all your sins and heals all your diseases, who redeems your life from the pit and crowns you with love and compassion . . . ." Psalm 103:3-4.

". . . As far as the east is from the west, so far has He removed our transgressions from us," Psalm 103:12.

". . . Though your sins are like scarlet, they shall be as white as snow; though they are red as crimson, they shall be like wool," Isaiah 1:18.

". . . Your guilt is taken away and your sins atoned for," Isaiah 6:7.

"I have swept away your offenses like a cloud, your sins like the morning mist . . . ." Isaiah 44:22.

"But He was pierced for our transgressions, He was crushed for our iniquities; the punishment that brought us peace was upon Him, and by His wounds we are healed," Isaiah 53:5.

". . . the Son of Man has the authority on earth to forgive sins . . . ." Matthew 9:6.

". . . Friend, your sins are forgiven," Luke 5:20.

"In Him we have redemption through His blood, the forgiveness of sins. . ." Ephesians 1:7.

"For He has rescued us from the dominion of darkness and brought us into the kingdom of the Son He loves, in whom we have redemption, the forgiveness of sins," Colossians 1:13-14 (NIV).

"And the prayer offered in faith will make the sick person well; the Lord will raise him up. If he has sinned, he will be forgiven. Therefore confess your sins to each other and pray for each other so that you may be healed," James 5:15-16.

"If we confess our sins, He is faithful and just and will forgive us our sins and purify us from all unrighteousness," I John 1:9.

". . . Your sins have been forgiven on account of His name," I John 2:12.

I AM

1. A Child of God (Romans 8:16)
2. Redeemed from the Hand of the Enemy (Psalm 107:2)
3. Forgiven (Colossians 1:13-14)
4. Saved by Grace Through Faith (Ephesians 2:8)
5. Justified (Romans 5:1)
6. Sanctified (I Corinthians 6:11)
7. A New Creature (II Corinthians 5:17)
8. Partaker of His Divine Nature (II Peter 1:4)
9. Redeemed from the Curse of the Law (Galatians 3:13)
10. Delivered from the Powers of Darkness (Colossians 1:13)
11. Led by the Spirit of God (Romans 8:14)
12. A Daughter/Son of God (Romans 8:14)
13. Kept in Safety Wherever I Go (Psalm 91:11)
14. Getting all my Needs Met by Jesus (Philippians 4:19)
15. Casting all my Cares on Jesus (I Peter 5:7)
16. Strong in the Lord and in the Power of His Might (Ephesians 6:10)
17. Doing all Things Through Christ who Strengthen Me (Philippians 4:13)
18. An Heir of God and Joint Heir with Jesus (Romans 8:17)
19. Heir to the Blessings of Abraham (Galatians 3:13-14)
20. Observing and Doing the Lord's Commandments (Deuteronomy 28:12)
21. Blessed Coming In and Going Out (Deuteronomy 28:6)
22. An Inheritor of Eternal Life (I John 5:11-12)
23. Blessed with all Spiritual Blessings (Ephesians 1:3)
24. Healed by His Stripes (I Peter 2:24)
25. Exercising my Authority over the Enemy (Luke 10:19)
26. Above only and not Beneath (Deuteronomy 28:13)
27. More than a Conqueror (Romans 8:37)
28. Establishing God's Word here on Earth (Matthew 16:19)
29. Overcomer by the Blood of the Lamb & Word of my Testimony (Rev. 12:11)
30. Daily Overcoming the Devil (I John 4:4)
31. Not Moved by What I See (II Corinthians 4:18)
32. Walking by Faith and not by Sight (II Corinthians 5:7)
33. Casting Down Vain Imaginations (II Corinthians 10:4-5)
34. Bringing Every Thought into Captivity (II Corinthians 10:5)
35. Being Transformed by a Renewed Mind (Romans 12:1-2)
36. A Laborer Together with God (I Corinthians 3:9)
37. The Righteousness of God in Christ (II Corinthians 5:21)
38. An Imitator of Jesus (Ephesians 5:1)
39. The Light of the World (Matthew 5:14)

Participant's Evaluation

Letting us know your feelings and opinion of our group will help you determine its value to you and help us better minister in future groups. Please use additional paper if more space is needed.

What were the reasons you came to the group?
_____

Do you feel you received healing in those areas?
_____

What issues do you feel are still unresolved?
_____

If you have unresolved issues, how will you seek to meet these?
_____

What did you like most about the group?
_____

What did you like least about the group?
_____

Would you be interested in attending another group?
_____

Would you like to meet with someone on an individual basis?
_____

Your name: _____ Date: _____

Your group leader's name: _____

Leader's Evaluation

Date:

Leader: Telephone: Email:

Co-leader: Telephone: Email:

<u>Group Performance</u>   <u>Ugh!</u>   <u>Fair</u>   <u>Great</u>

   Attendance?

   Members fully participated?

   Time used wisely?

   Effective prayer ministry?

Group Strengths:
_____

Group Weaknesses:
_____

What situations challenged you personally during this group?
_____

Were you able to discuss these situations with your advisor?
_____

In what way do you feel better equipped to handle a similar problem in the future?
_____

*Signature*_____

Notes

Notes

Notes

Notes

About the Author

With 25 years experience in prophetic counseling and pastoring, emotional healing and trauma resolution, Yvonne serves on Pastoral Counseling staff in the Transformation Center at Bethel Church in Redding, CA. She also ministers and travels with the Bethel Sozo team.

Yvonne is an author of 6 books, conference speaker, third-year Bethel School of Supernatural Ministry graduate, and hosts articles and Q/A column for the Christian Quarterly entitled *Talk With Yvonne*.

As an ordained minister, Yvonne's passion is to see people acquire their Kingdom identity, inheritance, intimacy and authority. She is available for speaking or personal ministry.

CONTACT

Yvonne Martinez

(530) 255-2099 x 1921

yvonnem@ibethel.org   or   talkwithyvonne@hotmail.com

Book and workbook available at www.StillwaterLavender.com

Bethel Church website: www.ibethel.org

Bethel Sozo website: www.bethelsozo.com

Made in the USA
Charleston, SC
15 October 2010